Getting Around In Christian Circles

"They devoted themselves to the apostles' teaching and to the fellowship, to the breaking of bread and to prayer. Everyone was filled with awe, and many wonders and miracles were done by the apostles. All the believers were together and had everything in common. Selling their possessions and goods, they gave to anyone as he had need. Every day they continued to meet together in the temple courts. They broke bread in their homes and ate together with glad and sincere hearts, praising God and enjoying the favor of all the people..."

- Acts 2: 42-47

Getting Around In Christian Circles

Jim Biscardi, Jr.

Getting Around In Christian Circles

Scripture quotations are taken from the Holy Bible, New International Version, Copyright 1973, 1978, 1984 by International Bible Society.

Scripture quotations marked KJV are taken from the King James Version of the Bible.

Special thanks to Rev. Grace Alfieri, Rev. Peter Lambo, and Joe Velez for their support and helpful suggestions. Thanks also to my wife, Patty, for her constant encouragement throughout this project.

Published by

Mantle Ministries
PO Box 248
Lanoka Harbor, NJ 08734

Cover Design: Faithlyn Robinson
Cover Photos: Dreamstime.com

TABLE OF CONTENTS

INTRODUCTION

As Christians we often encounter believers and unbelievers who are sincerely searching to understand truth. They ask what the Christian life is all about - how to keep their lives connected to Christ - how they can "see" Christ better - how to keep their lives pure and holy - how to increase faith - how to get their arms around The Book of Revelation – What church is really meant to be - and much more.

Getting Around In Christian Circles is a textbook of essential lessons – gleaned from 30 years of teaching adults - for successfully living the Christian life. Each of the topics is illustrated with circles to help aid understanding or add interest. Anybody can use these simple illustrations to help themselves and others understand and embrace the Christian life.

Besides lessons on Christian concepts and principles, this book also provides useful guides to church life, spiritual gifts and salvation, Christian ethics, and a glossary to help better understand the words and phrases frequently used in Christian circles. It also provides advice for recognizing and avoiding abuses in the church.

This book is especially useful as a teaching aid and can be an exceptional resource for pastors and Christian educators.

My sincere hope is that *Getting Around In Christian Circles* will prove to be a reliable guide for the reader as it has for me and many hundreds of Christ's disciples to help weather the storms of life, run the Christian race well, and help others to be successful.

- Jim Biscardi, Jr

"...I consider everything a loss compared to the surpassing greatness of knowing Christ Jesus my Lord...that I may gain Christ...I want to know Christ and the power of his resurrection and the fellowship of sharing in his sufferings, becoming like him in his death, and so, somehow, to attain to the resurrection from the dead."

- Philippians 3: 8-11

CHAPTER 1 – Transformed Into The Image Of Christ

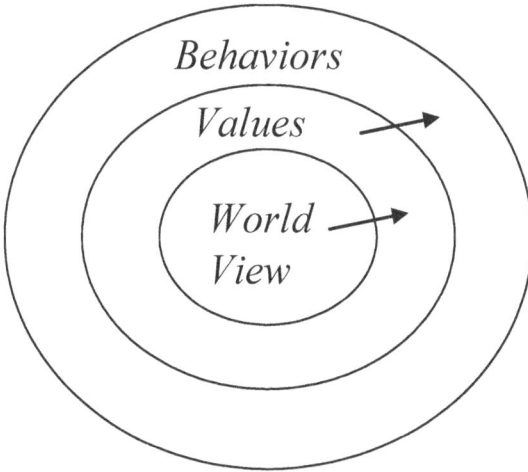

Before coming to Christ, our world view has SELF in the center. Whatever or whoever is in the center of our worldview (i.e. has the center of our attention) has us. It then shapes our values and our behaviors. This creates a model for living - all the rules for life and how we measure success.

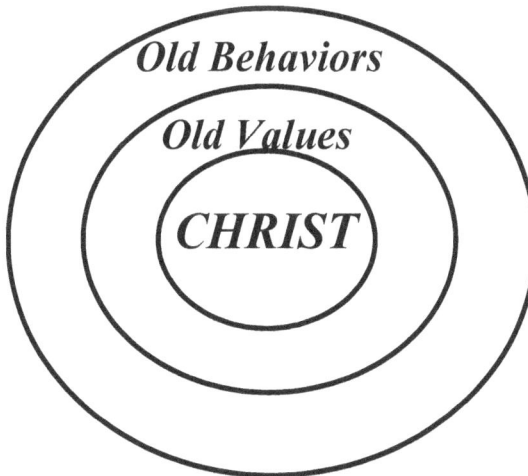

When we come to Christ, we realize that Christ must be in the center of our world view. But our old values and behaviors come along with us. If you don't believe this, an example is the apostle Peter in Acts 10, where he tells the Lord he will not eat unclean meat because he's learned never to do it. So the Lord's command meant nothing because of his old values. Also see Luke 5: 36-39, Jesus said, *"...new wine must be poured into new wineskins. And no one after*

drinking old wine wants the new, for he says, 'The old tastes better.'"

The Transformation

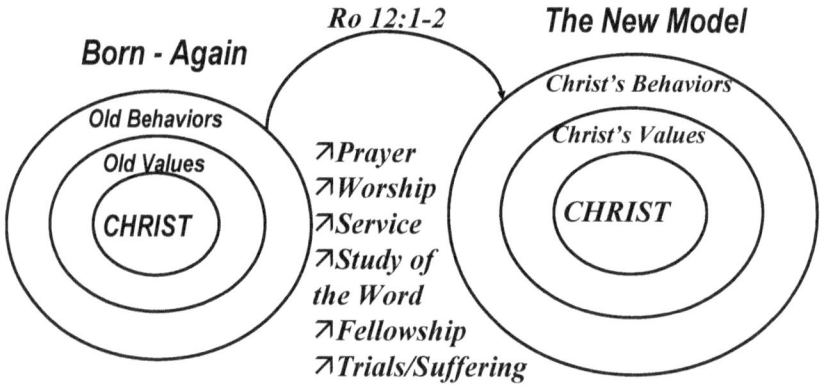

"Therefore, I urge you, brothers, in view of God's mercy, to offer yourselves as living sacrifices, holy, and pleasing to God – which is your spiritual worship. Do not conform any longer to the pattern of this world, but be transformed by the renewing of your mind. Then you will be able to test and approve what God's will is – his good, pleasing, and perfect will." (Romans 12: 1-2). When we come to Christ, our old model of values and behaviors comes with us. Over time, these values and behaviors are changed into a Christ-centered model with Christ in the center of our world view with Christ's values and behaviors. We are transformed by Studying the Word, Prayer, Worship, Fellowship, Service, and Trials/Suffering.

↗ Build self-esteem in others

↗ Recognize & reward good behavior

Pull-Don't Push
Mt 11:28

Servant Leader
Jn 13:14

Jesus Christ

↗ Open to the ideas of others - listening

↗ Building loyalty - Keep your word, Admit mistakes, Fight unfair, abusive, immoral practices, Give discipline when required. Reward only good behavior.

↗ Communicate well & involve others in planning

Wisdom From Above
Ja 3:17

Heart-to-Heart
Jn 10:3, 14
1Cor 9:19-22

↗ Honestly provide feedback to others on behavior

↗ Develop heart in people for serving others

↗ Build unity and family

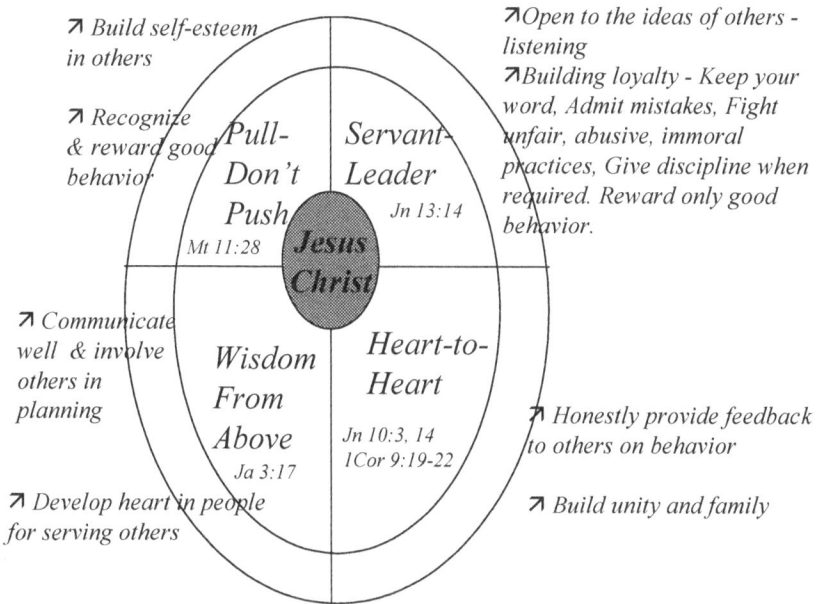

It's impossible to capture our Lord Jesus Christ's image in a simple diagram. This illustration depicts the essence of the Christ-like model with Christ's values and behaviors into which we are transformed over time.

Growth is faster both for us and others if we obey the Great Commission (Matthew 28:19) to make disciples and teach them. As Great Commission disciple-makers, we need to embrace the values and behaviors that make Christ great. The four values are found in the cross: **Servant Leader** means serving others – See Matthew 23:11 - the self sacrifice of the cross (John 3:16); **Heart-to-Heart** is making time to know others and allowing them to know us – the love of the cross (Romans 5:8); **Wisdom From Above** is "first pure" - See James 3:17 – the holiness of the cross (2Corinthians 5:21); **Pull-Don't–Push** means drawing people (Matthew 11:28) rather than pushing them - the humility and obedience of the cross (Philippians 2:7-8; Matthew 16:24).

"So God created man in his own image, in the image of God created he him; male and female created he them…And the Lord God commanded the man, saying, Of every tree of the garden thou mayest freely eat: But of the tree of the knowledge of good and evil, thou shalt not eat of it…for thou shalt surely die…And the serpent said unto the woman, Ye shall not surely die…ye shall be as gods knowing good and evil. The woman…took of the fruit, thereof, and did eat, and gave also unto her husband with her; and he did eat."

- Genesis 1:27, 2:16-17, 3:4-6 KJV

CHAPTER 2 – You And Your Old Man!

Natural Man

Adam Before The Fall

Natural Man

Old Man Under The Control Of Sin

Adam After The Fall

Consider what man was like when he was first created. He was a natural man – with body, soul, and spirit. This natural man, or the flesh as we call it, could act independently and make decisions. He had a free will, wisdom, skill, intellect, eloquence, feelings, etc. When Adam and Eve sinned, however, this natural man was subjected to what scripture calls the "old man". That's the part of us that loved to sin – enjoyed it. In fact, this natural man was not only influenced by sin, but also came into the bondage of sin. The natural man actually served sin. This verse (Romans 6:6 KJV) tells us what happens to this "old man" as a result of accepting the work of Christ. It says, *"...that our old man is crucified with him, that the body of sin might be destroyed, that henceforth we should not serve sin."*

The destruction done by the "old man" in our lives is like what locusts do to trees. When they attack a tree, they leave nothing of value on the tree. It's like a "hit and run" accident. They come in, and in 15 minutes eat up everything of value – even the bark. You go to sleep at night as a satisfied owner of a grove of productive trees. When you wake in the morning, your whole life is changed. You've lost everything – a victim of an unscrupulous predator that "hits and runs". Sin is like that. When sin comes in and is given full sway in a person's life, it leads to spiritual destruction of that life. Think of how drugs ruin people's lives. The same is true about sins of the mind (e.g. impure or unwise thoughts and big egos), and of the heart (e.g. wrong attractions, appetites, desires, and illicit sex). Sins of envy, greed, and other sorts also destroy lives.

It's like the old time clothes wringer that squeezed every drop of water out of the wet clothes. Sin saps every drop of sincerity, real caring, real truth and fulfillment out of a life – often without the person realizing it. Life is empty and ruined. Reality becomes believing one's own lies and calling good evil and evil good. The worst tragedy is that it separates us from the greatest lover ever known – our heavenly Father, who created us to enjoy fellowship with Him.

When We Are Born-Again, The Old Man In Us Is Crucified With Christ

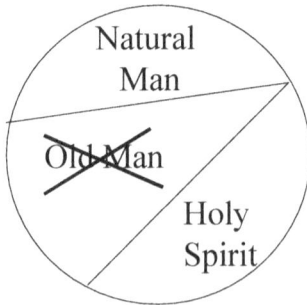

When we are "born-again", we are not only "saved" from the death sentence of eternal separation from God, but also delivered from the power of sin, itself. We are no longer in bondage to serve sin. We are set free to seek the kingdom of God and His righteousness. The "old man" in us that made us slaves to sin – that caused us to enjoy sinning – that convinced us that there was nothing wrong with what we were doing – is crucified with Christ (Romans 6:6). God, sending His Holy Spirit to dwell within us, gives us the power to overcome the temptation and attraction of sin and instead to produce pure "fruit". *"For when ye were servants of sin, ye were free from righteousness.   What fruit had ye then in those things whereof ye are now ashamed? For the end of those things is death. But now being made free from sin, and become servants of God, ye have your fruit unto holiness, and the end everlasting life."* (Romans 6:20-22 KJV).   *"...greater is He that is in you, than he that is in the world."* (1John 4:4 KJV).

That doesn't mean that we never sin – because our natural man is still alive in us.   It means, however, that when we sin the Holy Spirit is faithful to convict us – so that we want to tell God we're sorry for it.   And then because of Christ's sacrifice for our sin, *"He (can now be and) is faithful and just to forgive our sins, and to cleanse us from all unrighteousness."* (1John 1:9 KJV)

"But the Lord said to Samuel, 'Do not look at his appearance or at the height of his stature, because I have refused him. For the Lord does not see as a man sees; for man looks at the outward appearance, but the Lord looks at the heart.'"

- 1Samuel 16:7

CHAPTER 3 – Have You Taken Jesus Through Your Heart Lately?[1]

Jesus said, *"If a man loves me he will keep my words: and my Father will love him, and we will come and make our abode with him"* (John 14:23 KJV). So while Jesus is preparing a place for us in Heaven (John 14:3), we are to prepare a place for Him in our hearts.

To determine how we're doing, take Jesus through these rooms in your heart...

A Christian's heart has many rooms

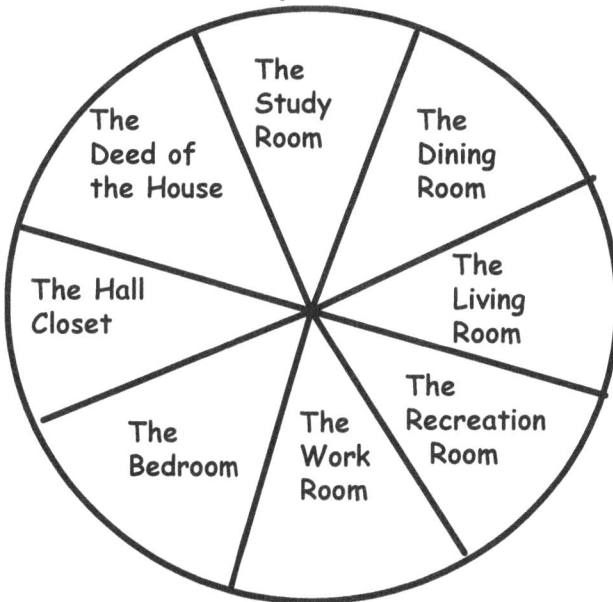

The Study Room

The Deed of the House

The Dining Room

The Hall Closet

The Living Room

The Bedroom

The Work Room

The Recreation Room

---

[1] Adapted from *My Heart, Christ's Home* – by Robert Boyd Munger, 1986

- **The Study** - What would Jesus see in your mind? What are the magazines and books we read, or the videos and TV programs we watch? He would want His picture in the center of that room and the books of the scriptures on all the book shelves.
- **The Dining Room** - What would you serve Jesus? What are your appetites and desires? Your education, wealth, investments, awards, etc.? If so, Jesus would not eat much and would say, *"My food is to do the will of him who sent me and to finish his work."* (John 4:34)
- **The Living Room** - This is the room where Jesus waits to meet with us everyday. Do you read the Word and pray to Him daily? He would tell us that that time is not just for us but also for Him. He paid a great price for us - and wants to meet and fellowship with us often.
- **The Recreation Room** - This is our place of fun and fellowship. Would the Lord find us taking Him with us when we go out with friends - or would we have to tell the Lord to wait home because He would feel uncomfortable? He would remind us that we were going to let Him be our Friend and go with us everywhere.
- **The Work Room** - The Lord would look to see what we've done for Him lately. We might say that we felt awkward and clumsy in spiritual things. He would agree and tell us to put ourselves in the control of the Holy Spirit and let Him lead us in doing God's work.
- **The Bedroom** - Here the Lord would remind us that He doesn't restrict sex to a marriage relationship because sex is bad but because it is good under the right conditions. When not in marriage, sex can be harmful and destructive.
- **The Hall Closet** - As we are showing Jesus around our heart, He may pass the hall closet and mention that there's a horrible odor coming from there - maybe some stuff left over from our lives before we asked Him to come in. He'd want us to clean it. We would tell Him that we didn't have the strength - these things are too hard for us to "set aside". But we'd finally ask Him to clean it for us. Jesus would

say that He'd been waiting for us to ask. Very soon the closet would be clean.

Then, one day, we ask the Lord to clean **our whole house** like He did the hall closet. He would say, "That's why I'm here. You can't live the Christian life alone. But I don't have the authority to clean your house because you've only made Me a guest here. First, you'll need to sign over the deed of your house to Me and make Me the owner." So we finally really do make Jesus Lord of our lives!

Have you ever met Christians who enjoy having Jesus as Savior but don't live like He's their Lord?   Could we, ourselves, be those Christians? As an illustration of those who never received Jesus as Lord, consider the Laodicean church of Revelation 3: 14-21. They were more interested in acquiring wealth and material possessions (Revelation 3:17) than to *"seek first his kingdom and his righteousness."* (Matthew 6: 33). They loved money so much that Jesus is pictured outside the church knocking on the church door - and on the hearts of its people – asking them to open the door to Him! (Revelation 3:20). They never accepted Him as Lord and eventually the house of their hearts became so cluttered with the things of this world that there was no room for Jesus even as a guest!!

" I am the true vine and my Father is the gardener. He cuts off every branch in me that bears no fruit, while every branch that does bear fruit he trims clean so that it will be even more fruitful…"

Jesus – John 15: 1-2

CHAPTER 4 - How To Keep Our Christian Life In Contact With Christa

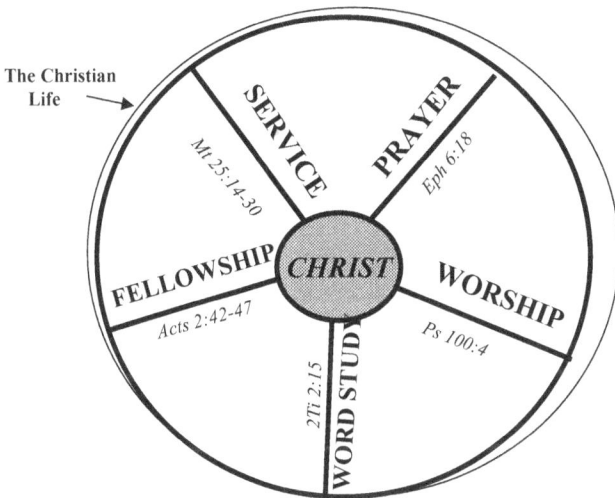

The Christian Life

THE CHRISTIAN LIFE IS LIKE RIDING A BICYCLE. The outside rim of the wheel is connected to the hub by means of spokes. The rim is our Christian life. The hub is Christ. Our Lord must remain in the center of our lives – have the center of our attention – for the wheel to work right! Only He is perfect, flawless to be the hub. Everything else has imperfections that cause trouble in our ride.

We need to keep our life connected to Christ by five very important spokes – PRAYER, STUDY OF THE WORD, WORSHIP, FELLOWSHIP WITH OTHER CHRISTIANS, and SERVICE (doing something with the spiritual gifts and talents that God has given every Christian).

The Christian life is not an easy life – but it is the abundant life. There are struggles for us all. Trials and suffering is another spoke on the wheel that keeps our lives connected to Christ. That spoke, however, is under God's control – not ours (1Peter 1:6-7). And He will work all things together for good to those who love Him –

those who are called according to His purposes. (Romans 8: 28). One thing He does is use our suffering to comfort others. (2 Corinthians 1:4).

But sometimes we cause our own problems and make the ride "bumpy" for several reasons:

1. As mentioned above, Christ must be in the center of our lives – we often put ourselves back in that place.
2. The spokes need to be kept in balance. Some of us love to worship but don't want to study the Word. Some love to study, but sharing their life in fellowship is uncomfortable. Remember, different size spokes cause a rough ride.
3. As the spokes get longer, pumping the bike to go far is easier because the wheel is bigger. But if the spokes are short, we have to pump hard to cover just a short distance because the wheel is small.

Here's an easy way to remember the spokes. Think of them as spiritual vitamins:

1. Vitamin A is the ASK vitamin – that's PRAYER.
2. Vitamin B is the BIBLE vitamin – that's STUDY THE WORD
3. Vitamin C is the COMFORT vitamin – that's the result of our TRIALS & SUFFERING
4. Vitamin D is the DO vitamin – that's SERVICE
5. Vitamin E is the EXALT vitamin – that's WORSHIP
6. Vitamin K is the KOINONIA vitamin – that's a Greek word that means FELLOWSHIP.

Jesus used a great illustration to teach us that we must stay connected with Him. He said, *"Remain in me, and I will remain in you. No branch can bear fruit by itself; it must remain in the vine. Neither can you bear fruit unless you remain in me. I am the vine; you are the branches. If a man remains in me and I in him, he will bear much fruit; apart from me you can do nothing."* (John 15:4-5)

CHAPTER 5 – What Do We Mean By "Fellowship?"

Fellowship in Christian circles does not mean socializing. It may start that way, but eventually it results in sharing our lives with one another and being accountable to each other.

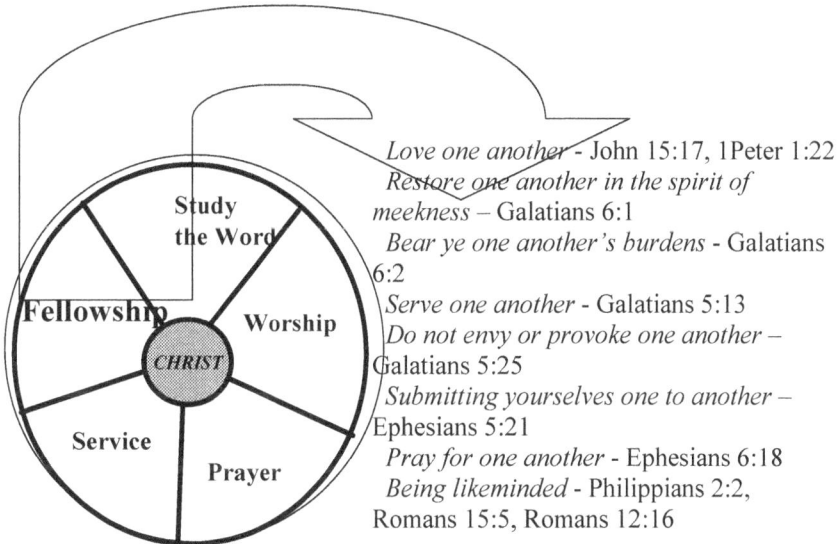

Love one another - John 15:17, 1Peter 1:22
Restore one another in the spirit of meekness – Galatians 6:1
Bear ye one another's burdens - Galatians 6:2
Serve one another - Galatians 5:13
Do not envy or provoke one another – Galatians 5:25
Submitting yourselves one to another – Ephesians 5:21
Pray for one another - Ephesians 6:18
Being likeminded - Philippians 2:2, Romans 15:5, Romans 12:16
Teach and admonish one another - Colossians 3:16
Forebearing one another and forgiving one another - Colossians 3:13
Comfort one another 2 Corinthians 1:4, 1 Thessalonians 4:18
Exhort (encourage) and edify one another - 1 Thessalonians 5:11
Greet one another - 2 Thessalonians 5:26
Receive one another - Romans 15:7
Be members one of another - Romans 12:4
Be kindly affectioned with brotherly love - Romans 12:10
Be tender-hearted one to another - Ephesians 4:32
Lay down our lives for one another - 1 John 3:16
Meet the needs of one another - 1 John 3:17

Sharing life means that we are able to talk about our victories and defeats, our appointments and disappointments, the good and bad in our lives. We can ask for prayer in a personal matter and be confident that the other person will not tell anyone else about our need or weakness. We help one another be built up in Christ by meeting often. And we're available to one another 24/7.

Commitment is essential for Christians to fellowship successfully. It's not optional.   Relating in the Body of Christ is outlined succinctly in the following verses: *"They devoted themselves to the apostles' teaching and to fellowship, to the breaking of bread and to prayer…All the believers were together and had everything in common. Selling their possessions and goods, they gave to anyone as he had need. Every day they continued to meet together in the temple courts. They broke bread in their homes and ate together with glad and sincere hearts, praising God and enjoying the favor of all the people. And the Lord added to their number daily those who were being saved."* (Acts 2: 42-27).

- Verse 42 – *"They devoted themselves to the apostles' teaching and to fellowship, to the breaking of bread and to prayer."*   We must remember the 30 "one another" scriptures – some of which are given above when we described "fellowship".   In general, they demonstrate the interdependence between Christians.   They also describe times when we need to confront our brethren (e.g. restore, forgive, teach, admonish, and exhort one another).
- Verses 44-45 – *"All believers were together and had everything in common.   Selling their possessions and goods, they gave to anyone as he had need."*   Christians need to learn that God has set us in the Body to enable everyone's need to be satisfied. This is a very practical part of a Christian's life!
- Verse 46 – *"Every day they continued to meet together in the temple courts. They broke bread in their homes and ate together with glad and sincere hearts."*   The commitment was not just a Sunday or mid-week handshake.
- Verse 47 – *"praising God and enjoying the favor of all the people.   And the Lord added to their number daily those who were being saved."*   This way of relating to one another produces results for evangelism.

Most of us don't appreciate the value of fellowship.   Until our flesh is dealt with by the Holy Spirit, we find it easy and natural to go it alone. Let me illustrate this point by considering the life of Jacob.[2] In the early days of Jacob's life, he lived by his cunning and deceit – he didn't think he needed anyone – not even God. He stole his brother's birthright (Genesis 25:31-34). He lied to his father (Genesis 27:19). He even devised a plan that would make himself rich in livestock while he bankrupted his uncle Laban's business (Genesis 30:37-42) – even though Laban tricked and deceived Jacob many times.

After 20 years of working for Laban, Jacob heard God call him to return to fellowship with his father and family. Even though the Lord protected him from Laban and showed him a band of angels that would watch over him (Genesis 31:55 – 32:2), when he heard that Esau was coming, still Jacob felt the need to devise a cunning plan to escape his brother's wrath. He still depended only on his own wits. But on his journey back, when Jacob was all alone at Peniel, scripture says that an Angel (possibly Christ) wrestled with him all night. Now Jacob's natural strength (i.e. his flesh) was so strong that he almost prevailed (Genesis 32:25) until the Angel touched him in his thigh and crippled him.

Now Jacob's flesh was truly weakened, and the Angel could not leave him because he depended on the Angel. So Jacob held him close and wouldn't let him go; and he asked the Angel for a blessing. The Angel changed his name to Israel (Genesis 32: 28). Just like Jacob, we also have a "thigh" – a central "nerve-center" from where all our short comings emanate – that must be touched by God. Until we are weakened, we don't find it necessary to hold onto Christ (2Corinthians 12:10). When people saw Jacob's limp (not just what came from his lips), they knew he was changed. When they see our "limp", they'll know we've been changed also.

After reconciling with his brother, Jacob (now Israel) moved on to Shechem where he built an altar called El – elohe-Israel (the God of Israel). Still God was only Israel's God. (Genesis 33: 16-20).

---

[2] Adapted from "Changed Into His Likeness", Watchman Nee, Victory Press, 1967

Many of us Christians live like it's just "God and me." Then God called him to Bethel (which means God's House). It's God's home, the place where His power is seen through the Body of Christ. Jacob called the altar El – beth – el (God of Bethel). (Genesis 35: 2-3, 7). Jacob had moved from individualism to relatedness in the Body. In the Church, God is the God of Bethel not just "my God." Finally, Jacob was ready to move to Hebron (Genesis 35:27) and to come to his father Isaac. Hebron represents fellowship, mutuality, the place where nothing can be done individually or in isolation (1Corinthians 12: 14-30).

Until the flesh is dealt with – like with Jacob's flesh – we don't value fellowship. Until that happens, we're not ready to receive Christ from others – which is what fellowship is all about.

CHAPTER 6 – Why Does God Identify Himself As The God of Abraham, Isaac, And Jacob?

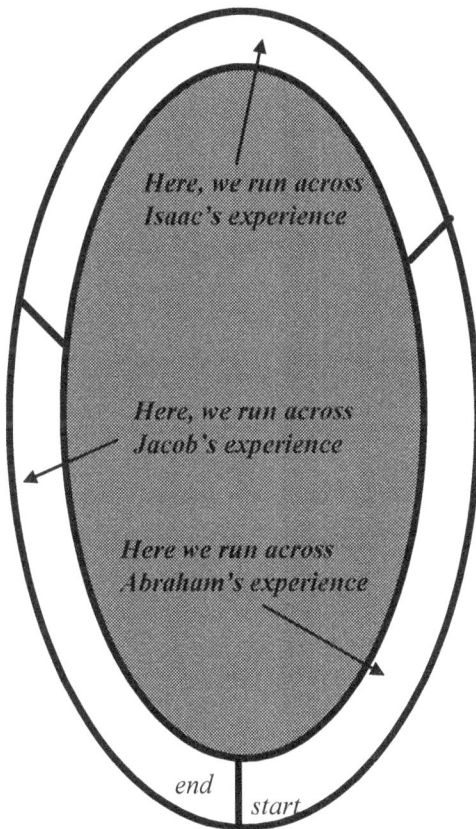

Here, we run across Isaac's experience

Here, we run across Jacob's experience

Here we run across Abraham's experience

end   start

"...since we are surrounded by such a great cloud of witnesses, let us throw off everything that hinders and the sin that so easily entangles, and let us run with perseverance the race marked out for us..." (Hebrews 12:1)

"I am the God of thy father, the God of Abraham, the God of Isaac, and the God of Jacob." (Exodus 3:6 KJV)

"But concerning the resurrection of the dead, have you not read what was spoken to you by God saying, 'I am the God of Abraham, the God of Isaac, and the God of Jacob'? God is not the God of the dead but of the living." (Matthew 22:31-32)

God identifies Himself to us as the God of these specific three patriarchs because (as we run the Christian race), it is the combined experience of these three men that defines the race run by all God's people on earth.

1. **ABRAHAM** learned that God is the true originator, from whom all of His new creation comes. We all have to learn that we can originate nothing. (1Peter 1:3-5). God is the one who begins everything. He originates new life and preserves it. Nothing that originated from Abraham, including Ishmael - the son of his flesh - could serve God's purpose. God is the Father – The Source. Learning this lesson, we begin to be the "people of God".

2. **ISAAC** illustrates the work of God in Christ towards us. We have "the adoption of sons". (Galatians 4:4-6). God is also the Son, the Giver. Isaac teaches us that we have nothing that we were not <u>given</u> - nothing is by our <u>attaining.</u> Isaac was born into wealth - we do not progress/advance into wealth - we are born into it. We need only receive.

3. **JACOB** shows us that our "natural strength" so dominates us that enjoying God's inheritance depends upon the "touch of God" on that natural strength. It (i.e. natural strength) in us competes with Christ in us and must be reduced to zero. The experience of how this happens in Jacob illustrates the disciplinary work of the Holy Spirit in our lives. (See Genesis chapters 28-49, especially Genesis 32:24-31, and the preceding chapter of this book).

CHAPTER 7 – The Christian Race. How Are You Running?

"Not as though I had already attained, either were already perfect: but this one thing I do, forgetting what is behind, and reaching forth to those things that are before, I press toward the mark for the prize of the high calling of God in Christ Jesus." (Philippians 3: 12-14 KJV)

"...I press toward the mark for the prize.."

- **What track are we on?** Career track? Ego track? Investment track? OR high calling track?
- **What equipment are we wearing?** Armor of God, including feet shod with "good news shoes" that bring peace? OR shoes with pointed tips that hurt fellow runners?
- **The path is full of potholes** - but we let God pour suffering into us so we can comfort other runners with the comfort God gives us (2 Corinthians 1:4).
- **How are we running?** By faith or by sight? Remember faith is our response to God's love. It can be seen by what we do. As you run, remember Romans 8:28.
- **How are we progressing?** Crawling? Walking? Running? Long distance racers "kick" hardest when they can see the finish line. Christians crawl because

they have a "fuzzy" view of the finish line AND the prize.

- **What's the prize?** Is it Heaven? Is it prospering here on earth? Is it to get one or more of the five crowns? Is it to get the biggest mansion in Heaven? NO. The prize is to be like Christ - *"to know Him in resurrection power and in His suffering"* (Philippians 3: 10).

- **Who wins the Christian race?** Do you try to beat me to the finish line? Do we compete with each other to win. NO. We all win TOGETHER - and help each other finish well. See Ephesians 2.

- This is the only race where **the spectators join the runners because of the WAY they see them running together in unity** (John 17:21). If we want to see the "great cloud of witnesses", look around us in church.

- **Where is the finish line?** Is it when we die? NO. It's when *"we shall all appear (together) before the judgment seat of Christ"* to be judged on how we ran the race (2 Corinthians 5:10).

- **Will our race be determined to be wood, hay, or stubble?** OR silver, gold, and precious stones - the stuff that the NEW JERUSALEM is made out of?

- **We can't run this race looking backwards** to past accomplishments. *"...forgetting those things that are behind, and reaching forth ...I press toward the...prize..."* (Philippians 3:13-14 KJV)

- **Stay on God's race track**...Romans 12: 1-2 cautions us not to be conformed to the pattern of this world and its values, but to be transformed by the renewing of our mind. When we come to Christ, we carry with us worldly values. Here are some of those values:
  o Be independent. Don't depend on others.
  o Take care of yourself – nobody else will.
  o Lead – don't follow.
  o Let others serve you. Don't serve anyone.
  o Get to know only people who can get you ahead.

- o Don't tell people too much about yourself.
- o Use people – love things.
- o To be respected as a leader, throw your weight around.
- o The end justifies the means. Motives don't count.
- o Getting is better than giving.

Here's a more complete portrait of the **World's track vs. God's track.**

* Adapted from "Commitment to a Local Expression of The Body of Christ", Larry Tomczak & C.J. Mahaney, 1978

Kingdom of the World
Satan - The god of this world (2COR 4:4)

Kingdom of God
Jesus is Lord! (PH 2:11)

Stay on God's racetrack.

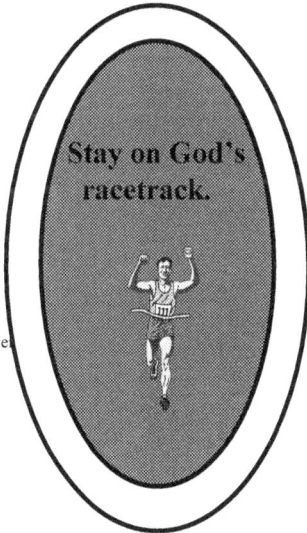

Kingdom of the World	Kingdom of God
• Seeing is believing	• Believing is seeing (JN 20:29)
• Wise	• Fool (1COR 3:18)
• Save your life	• Lose your life (MT 16:25)
• First	• Last (MK 9:35)
• Great	• Least (MK 10:43)
• Ruler	• Servant (MK 10:43)
• Exalted	• Humble Yourself (LK 14:11)
• Look to your own interests	• Look to others' interests. Count others better than self (PH 2:3)
• Get much	• Give much (LK 6:38)
• Make your good deeds known	• Keep your good deeds secret (MT 6:3)
• Love is feeling & conditional	• Love is commitment & unconditional (JN 15:12-13)
• Love grows cold	• Love never fails (1COR 13:8)
• Hate your enemies	• Love your enemies (MT 5:44)
• Retaliate	• Forgive (COL 3:13)
• Human might and human power	• Not by might/power but by my Spirit (ZECH 3:6)
• Eat, drink, and be merry	• Man doesn't live by bread alone (MT 4:4)
• It is impossible	• Everything is possible (MK 9:23)
• Check your stars	• Search the scriptures (JN 5:39)
• Bible was written by man	• Bible inspired by God (2TI 3:16)
• Bible is outdated	• My words shall never pass away (MT 24:35)
• Jesus was a good man	• Jesus is Lord! (PH 2:11)
• Jesus is dead	• Jesus Christ the same yesterday, today, and forever! (HE 13:8)
• Jesus is not coming again	• I will come again and take you (JN 14:3)

"Let us fix our eyes on Jesus, the Pioneer and Perfecter of our faith, who for the joy set before him endured the cross, scorning its shame, and sat down at the right hand of the throne of God. Consider him who endured such opposition from sinful men, so that you will not grow weary and lose heart."

- Hebrews 12: 2-3

CHAPTER 8 – The Gospel Of John Is Sight For Sore Eyes

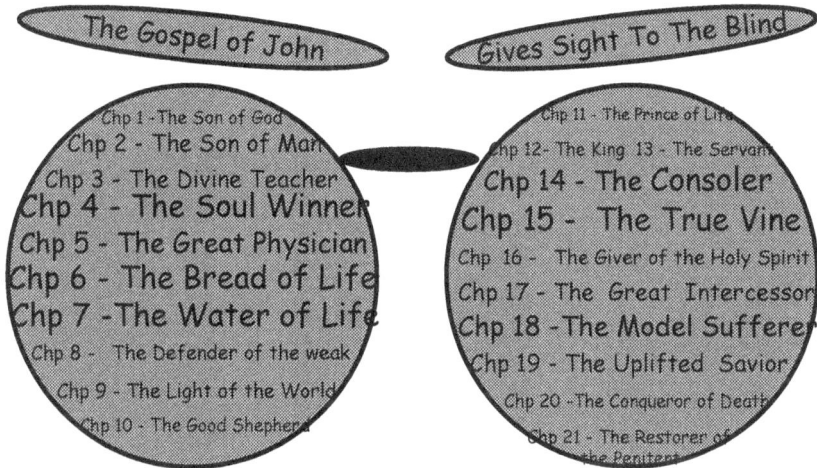

The Gospel of John is specially designed to help us get to know our Lord Jesus Christ better. Each chapter presents Him in a unique aspect of who He is. I received Jesus as my Lord and Savior after reading John 10 about how He is The Good Shepherd and knows His sheep and is known by them - that made me <u>see</u> how the Lord wanted a personal relationship with me.

When someone is seeking to know more about the Christian life, let them read this Gospel first - it will help them <u>see</u> Christ more clearly and completely.

The apostle Paul and the prophet Isaiah present their own portraits of Christ. Here's some help to "see" those pictures...[3]

---

[3] Adapted from The New Chain-Reference Bible, Kirkbride Bible Co., 1964

Paul's Pictures of Christ

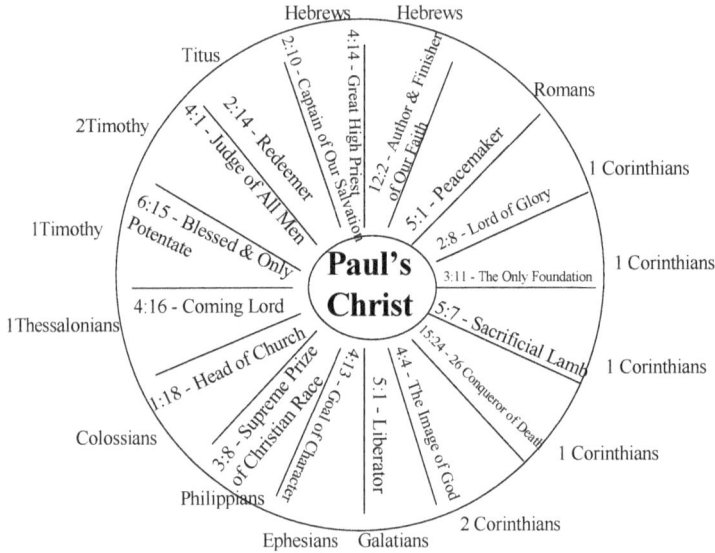

Hebrews — 4:14 - Great High Priest
Hebrews — 12:2 - Author & Finisher of Our Faith
Titus — 2:10 - Captain of Our Salvation
2Timothy — 2:14 - Redeemer
4:1 - Judge of All Men
1Timothy — 6:15 - Blessed & Only Potentate
1Thessalonians — 4:16 - Coming Lord
Colossians — 1:18 - Head of Church
Philippians — 3:8 - Supreme Prize of Christian Race
Ephesians — 4:13 - Goal of Character
Galatians — 5:1 - Liberator

Paul's Christ

Romans — 5:1 - Peacemaker
1 Corinthians — 2:8 - Lord of Glory
1 Corinthians — 3:11 - The Only Foundation
1 Corinthians — 5:7 - Sacrificial Lamb
1 Corinthians — 15:24-26 Conqueror of Death
1 Corinthians — 4:4 - The Image of God
2 Corinthians

Book of Isaiah - Portrait of Christ

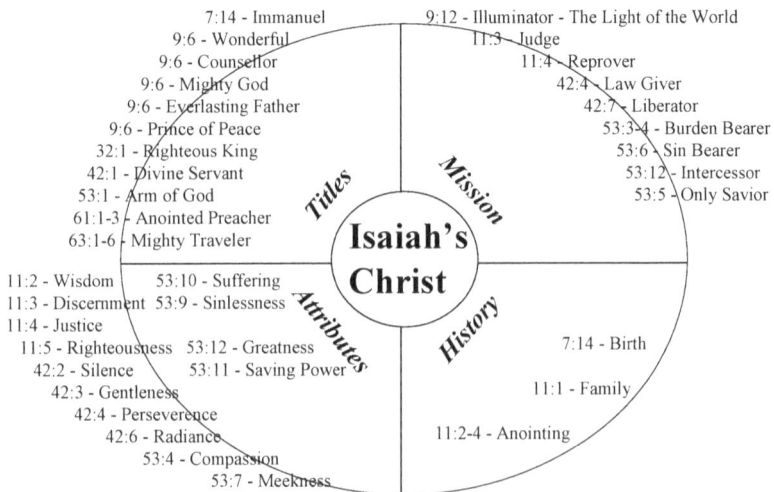

Isaiah's Christ

Titles
7:14 - Immanuel
9:6 - Wonderful
9:6 - Counsellor
9:6 - Mighty God
9:6 - Everlasting Father
9:6 - Prince of Peace
32:1 - Righteous King
42:1 - Divine Servant
53:1 - Arm of God
61:1-3 - Anointed Preacher
63:1-6 - Mighty Traveler

Mission
9:12 - Illuminator - The Light of the World
11:3 - Judge
11:4 - Reprover
42:4 - Law Giver
42:7 - Liberator
53:3-4 - Burden Bearer
53:6 - Sin Bearer
53:12 - Intercessor
53:5 - Only Savior

Attributes
11:2 - Wisdom   53:10 - Suffering
11:3 - Discernment   53:9 - Sinlessness
11:4 - Justice
11:5 - Righteousness 53:12 - Greatness
42:2 - Silence   53:11 - Saving Power
42:3 - Gentleness
42:4 - Perseverence
42:6 - Radiance
53:4 - Compassion
53:7 - Meekness

History
7:14 - Birth
11:1 - Family
11:2-4 - Anointing

CHAPTER 9 – What Is Man That God Is Mindful Of Him?

What is it about man that makes us so unique in God's creation? There's something that is beyond belief were it not for God's magnificent grace. It's that we can even claim to be a friend of God! Jesus told His disciples, *"You are my friends if you do what I command. I no longer call you servants because a servant does not know his master's business. Instead I have called you friends, for everything I learned from my Father, I have made known to you."* (John 15:14-15). Psalm 8:4 says, *"What is man that thou art mindful of him?"* In Genesis 1:26, *"God said, Let us create man in our image, after our likeness..."*

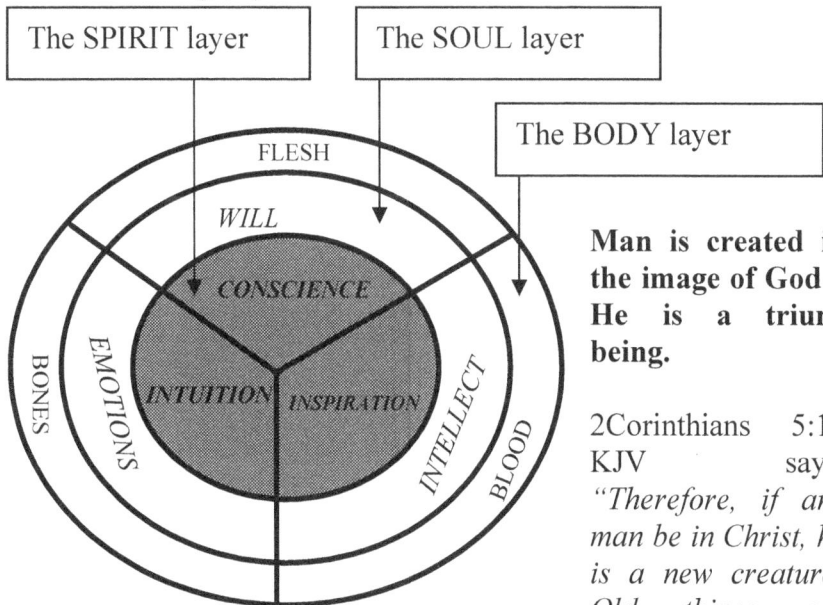

The SPIRIT layer

The SOUL layer

The BODY layer

Man is created in the image of God – He is a triune being.

2Corinthians 5:17 KJV says, *"Therefore, if any man be in Christ, he is a new creature: Old things are passed away; behold, all things are become new."*

WHAT HAPPENS WHEN MAN IS "BORN-AGAIN?" When we repent of our sins, and receive Jesus Christ and His sacrifice on the cross for forgiveness of our sins, then we are born - not of man or of the will of the flesh - but born of God. We are called "born-again."(John 1:12-13).   We are said to be *"born of the Spirit"* (John 3:8). The Holy Spirit takes up residence within our spirit. We are "new creations" because the Holy Spirit makes us into someone who has never existed before.   We used to be unique creations, but now we are a brand new member of God's family. Just like the blood is common that flows in the veins of physical family members, likewise the Holy Spirit is common in all Christians and makes us members of God's family. Also see the following scriptures about being "born-again": Romans 3:23; 5:12; 5:8; 6:23; 10:13; 10:9-11. See also Chapter 16, Guide To Spiritual Gifts And A Roadmap To Salvation.

The Holy Spirit works to change us into Christ's image by working outward - especially in our spirit and soul.   Even though all Christians have the Spirit - and are thereby part of God's family -

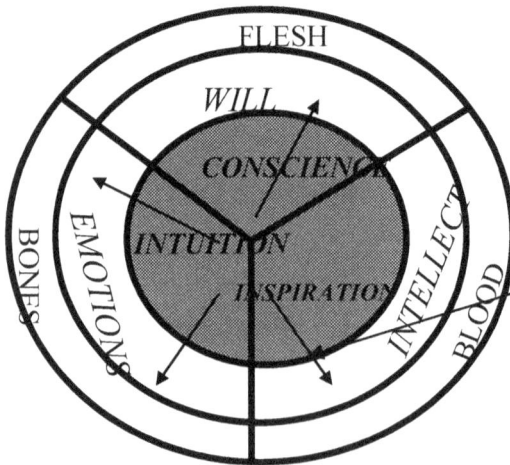

the Holy Spirit doesn't have all of us.   The natural man in us competes with the Spirit and must be reduced to zero.

Here's where the Holy Spirit lives in us (in our spirit). Jesus said that the Spirit would lead us into all truth.   To do that, He uses our STUDYING THE WORD, PRAYER, WORSHIP, FELLOWSHIP, PERFORMING A SERVICE FOR CHRIST, and COMFORTING OTHERS in their trials with the comfort we received from God during our own trials and suffering.   This process is called Christian "growth" or becoming mature in Christ.

A WORD ABOUT OUR CONSCIENCE. Our conscience is that inner voice or awareness that tells us if we are pleasing or displeasing God.   Hebrews 9:14 and 10:22 say that Christ has cleansed our conscience from sinfulness and sensitized it to serve

God. The Holy Spirit brings our conscience to life. We now have the responsibility to keep it pure. Paul declared, *"I have lived in all good conscience before God until this day"* (Acts 23:1). This is Paul's bold and consistent claim (Romans 9:1; 1Corinthians 4:4; 2Corinthians 1:12; 2Timothy 1:3). Dare we say with the same boldness and consistency, "My conscience is clear. I have lived a life of moral honesty and integrity?"[4]

---

[4] Our Daily Bread, RBC Ministries, October 21, 2006

"And without faith it is impossible to please God, because anyone who comes to him must believe that he exists and that he rewards those who diligently seek him."

- Hebrews 11:6

CHAPTER 10 – What Is Faith?

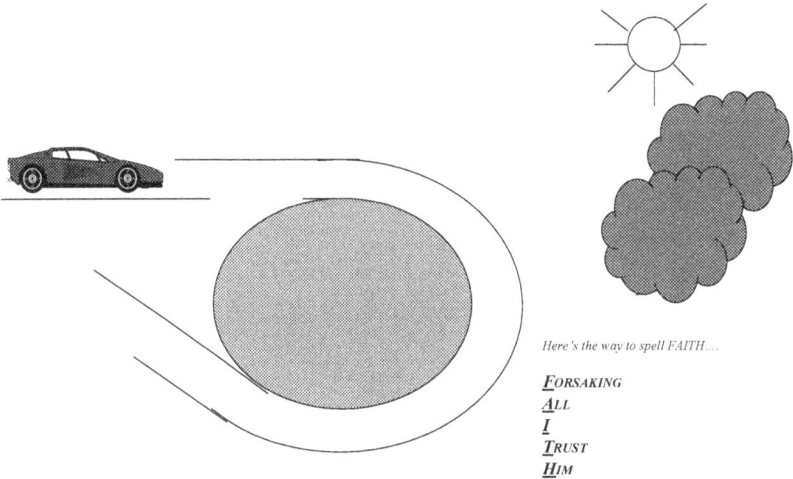

Here's the way to spell FAITH....

_F_ORSAKING
_A_LL
_I_
_T_RUST
_H_IM

"Now faith is the substance of things hoped for, the evidence of things not seen." (Hebrews 11:1 KJV)

Every morning, while driving to work, I come to a circle. Somewhere around that circle, during every season, at about the same time every morning, I will usually see the sun. There are times, however, that there are so many clouds in the sky that the sun is blocked from my view - but I know it's still there.

There will be times in your life as a Christian when troubles, trials, the stress of a situation, a prayer that goes unanswered for a long time, or even the injustice you see around you, block your clear view of Christ. Be assured, He is still there. _"...because God has said, 'Never will I leave you; never will I forsake you.'"_ (Hebrews 13:5). He is always working things together for the good of those who love Him (Romans 8:28). At those times, He is still faithfully waiting to commune with us.

THE MEASURE OF OUR FAITH

Is there a way to measure faith?   How do we observe faith? Remember this definition: **faith is our response to God's love.** It's what we <u>do</u> – not just what we say. The Scripture tells us not to be just hearers of the Word but doers! (James 1:22).   Jesus laid down His life for us.   And we show our faith in Him by laying down our lives for our brothers. (1 John 3:16).   *"Dear children, let us not love with words or tongue but with actions and in truth."*   (1 John 3:18).   *"What good is it, my brothers, if a man claims to have faith but has no deeds?   Can such faith save him?   ...In the same way, faith by itself, if it is not accompanied by action, is dead."* (James 2:14-17).   So we <u>can</u> measure and observe our faith by our deeds.

Once, when Jesus was in a boat with His disciples, He judged their faith as falling short: *"Then he got into the boat and his disciples followed him.   Without warning, a furious storm came up on the lake, so that the waves swept over the boat.   But Jesus was sleeping.   The disciples went and woke him, saying, 'Lord, save us! We're going to drown!'   He replied, 'You of little faith, why are you so afraid?'   Then he got up and rebuked the winds and the waves, and it was completely calm."*   (Matthew 8:23-26).   Their response (and ours) in the storm should have been to believe and trust Christ.

At another occasion, Jesus told His disciples that with just a mustard seed of faith, nothing would be impossible for them.   They could move and remove mountains. (Matthew 17:20).   Faith sees past the mountains – past all obstacles – and believes that what is hoped for is there beyond the mountain just waiting.   So faith keeps on going, persevering when others have quit trying, believing the goal is attainable – the prize just one more short step ahead.   If those clouds weren't there, the Sun (or the Son) would be revealed – because He is faithful and His promises are sure.

Forsaking **A**ll **I** **T**rust **H**im!   That's F.A.I.T.H.

CHAPTER 11 – What's The Key That Unlocks The Book of Revelation?

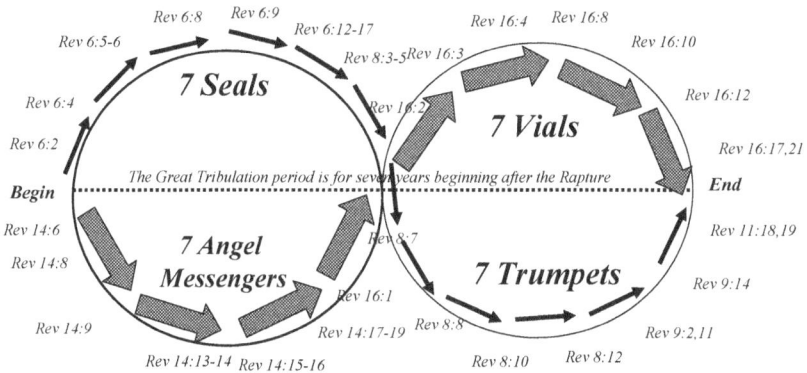

The key to unlocking the Book of Revelation is Gen 41:25-32. Joseph interpreted Pharaoh's dream. The dream was in two parts but each part complemented and confirmed the other. So the

	Seals	Trumpets	Angel Messengers	Vials
1	Rev 6:2	Rev 8:7	Rev 14:6	Rev 16:2
2	Rev 6:4	Rev 8:8	Rev 14:8	Rev 16:3
3	Rev 6:5-6	Rev 8:10	Rev 14:9	Rev 16:4
4	Rev 6:8	Rev 8:12	Rev 14:13-14	Rev 16:8
5	Rev 6:9	Rev 9:2,11	Rev 14:15-16	Rev 16:10
6	Rev 6:12-17	Rev 9:14	Rev 14:17-19	Rev 16:12
7	Rev 8:3-5	Rev 11:18,19	Rev 16:1	Rev 16:17,21

dream was actually one dream – not two. Joseph told Pharaoh that the dream was doubled because <u>God would soon bring it to pass</u>. In the very first verse, Revelation 1:1, and throughout the last chapter, Revelation 22:6, 7, 12, and 19, there are references to this revelation happening <u>quickly</u>. So, like Pharaoh's dream, the Book of Revelation is doubled but it is one revelation. The Seals & the Trumpets tell the whole story - so do the Angel Messengers and the Vials. Each of the two parts complements and confirms the other part.

Other key points from the Book of Revelation:

- Jesus rates churches - not just people (Rev 2&3).
- We, like the elders in Rev 4:11, will cast at Jesus' feet the crowns that we receive at the Judgment Seat of Christ. (2 Corinthians 5:10).
- We will carry through eternity the Mt of Transfiguration glory light of Dan 12:3 KJV – *"And they that be wise shall shine as the brightness of the firmament; and they that turn many to righteousness as the stars for ever and ever."* His name shall be in our foreheads (Revelation 22:4). What name? The name Jesus gave Himself – The Light of the World. In John 8: 12 KJV, Jesus said of Himself, *"I am the light of the world: he that followeth me shall not walk in darkness but have the light of life."* Speaking of the New Jerusalem and the saints, Revelation 22:5 KJV says, *"And there shall be no night there; and they need no candle, neither light of the sun; <u>for the Lord will give them light</u>: and they shall reign for ever and ever."*
- We return with Christ to the Battle of Armageddon bearing that light – like tiny stars following the Sun of Righteousness. We will look like Christ's mantle of tiny flowing lights (Ps 104:3) following behind Him. Then what God told Abraham in Genesis 15:6 KJV will become literally true, *"And [God] brought [Abraham] forth abroad, and said, Look now toward heaven, and tell the stars, if thou be able to number them: and he said unto him, So shall they seed be."*

CHAPTER 12 – The City Whose Builder And Maker Is God - Our Final Victory Lap

The victory lap for Christians is called "The New Jerusalem". It's the future home for all of God's people from where we will rule and reign with Him. I like to call it "Honeymoon City" because God and we will dwell together and we shall see Him face to face forever. *"...the throne of God and of the Lamb shall be in it; and his servants shall serve him: And they shall see his face; and his name shall be in their foreheads. And there shall be no night there; and they need no candle, neither the light of the sun; for the Lord God giveth them light: and they shall reign for ever and ever."* (Revelation 22:3-5 KJV) It's "Honeymoon City" also because the angel who was showing it to John told him that this city was prepared as a bride adorned for her husband (Revelation 21:2).

My favorite name for it, however, is "Showcase City" because – like the winner of the race who runs the victory lap - God will have us on display like sparkling jewels (Daniel 12:3) for the whole universe to see the glorious and redemptive work of Christ. The crowds that once competed with Christ (and us) and shouted for us to glorify "self" and follow the world, the flesh, and the devil, will be gone. In their place will be a "cloud of witnesses" throughout the universe who will constantly bask in the light of "Showcase City". They will shout the praises of God and His Christ as they are eternally reminded of God's awesome, magnificent victory!

Some might ask, "Who in the universe will be there to see this great display – the Bride of the Lamb – the City of God's precious love?" Who will be cheering the Victor and victors? We know that the angels will be there, but who else? *"And the nations of them which are saved shall walk in the light of it [i.e. New Jerusalem]: and the kings of the earth do bring their glory and honor into it. And the gates of it shall not be shut at all by day: for there shall be no night there. And they shall bring the glory and honor of the nations into it."* (Revelation 21:24-26 KJV) There will be surviving nations who did not fall for the deceit of Satan after he was loosed from his thousand-year imprisonment! These nations will be those we will *"rule and reign for ever and ever"*.

How could a city be "adorned" to be a bride? And how could it be a showcase? Let's look at the New Jerusalem. The Church is housed there – all the born-again believers from all time. They adorn its streets. We shall be shining like the stars in the firmament (Daniel 12:3). The degree of radiance will be determined at the Judgment Seat of Christ. In a way, we'll be like the precious stones that form the foundation of the City (Revelation 21:19-21). Precious stones that have been cut and shaped in the "heat" of this wondrous race our Father, through Christ, has given us to run by the power of the Holy Spirit. The names of the twelve tribes of Israel, the descendants of those fore-runners Abraham, Isaac, and Jacob, are inscribed at each of the

The Pearl of Great Price

twelve entrance gates (Revelation 21:12). And each of these gates were made of a ***single pearl*** (Revelation 21:21) – like "the pearl of great price" Jesus spoke about – which represents Christ Himself. The only way into the City is through Christ – the Entrance. *"...the kingdom of heaven is like unto a merchant man, seeking goodly pearls: Who, when he had found **one pearl** of great price, went and sold all that he had, and bought it."* (Matthew 13:45-46 KJV)

The foundations of the City have the names of the Lamb's twelve Apostles inscribed there (Revelation 21:14).   And the streets are of purest gold like transparent glass (Revelation 21:21) – gold that Peter said was the precious faith of believers when it was tried with fire (1Peter 1: 7). Finally, this City has "the glory of God: and her light was like unto a stone most precious, even like a jasper stone, clear as crystal." (Revelation 21:11) It was like a great glass case that contained the precious jewels of the Lord being displayed for the entire universe for ever and ever as a final victory lap of those who ran for their life God's way.

In the New Jerusalem, the tree of life is eaten freely. People live as God intended from the beginning with no more curse from sin (Revelation 22:3). God's home is with men and He shall wipe away all tears from their eyes. There shall be no more death, nor sorrow, nor crying, nor shall there be any more pain. The former things will all pass away and God will make everything new. (Revelation 21: 4-5)

"I come quickly; and my reward is with me to give to every man according as his work shall be." (Revelation 22:12, 20 KJV) *"The Spirit and the bride say Come. And let him that heareth say, Come. And let him that is athirst come. And whosoever will, let him take the water of life freely."* (Revelation 22:17 KJV).

"Let us hold fast the confession of our hope without wavering, for He who promised is faithful. And let us consider one another in order to stir up love and good works, not forsaking the assembling of ourselves together, as is the manner of some, but exhorting one another, and so much the more as you see the Day approaching."

- Hebrews 10: 23-25 KJV

CHAPTER 13 - A Christian's Guide To Church Life

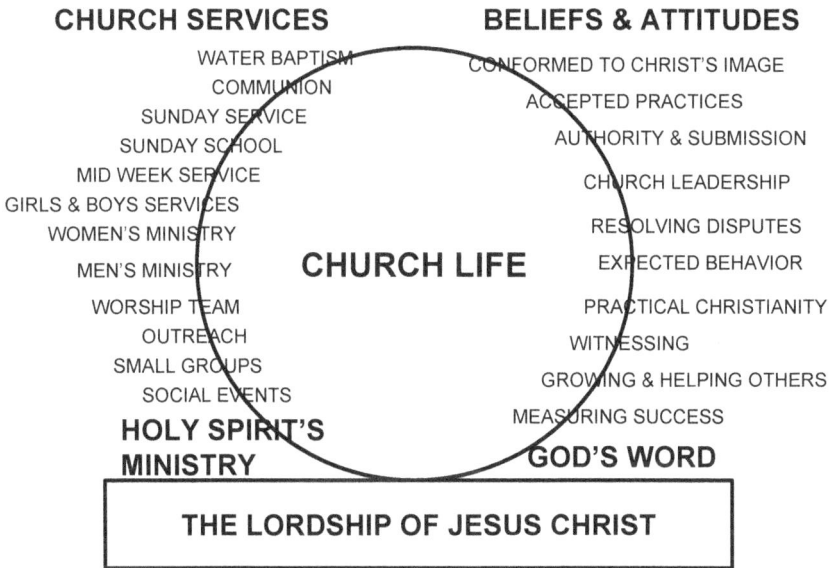

CHURCH SERVICES

BELIEFS & ATTITUDES

WATER BAPTISM
COMMUNION
SUNDAY SERVICE
SUNDAY SCHOOL
MID WEEK SERVICE
GIRLS & BOYS SERVICES
WOMEN'S MINISTRY
MEN'S MINISTRY
WORSHIP TEAM
OUTREACH
SMALL GROUPS
SOCIAL EVENTS

CONFORMED TO CHRIST'S IMAGE
ACCEPTED PRACTICES
AUTHORITY & SUBMISSION
CHURCH LEADERSHIP
RESOLVING DISPUTES
EXPECTED BEHAVIOR
PRACTICAL CHRISTIANITY
WITNESSING
GROWING & HELPING OTHERS
MEASURING SUCCESS

CHURCH LIFE

HOLY SPIRIT'S MINISTRY

GOD'S WORD

THE LORDSHIP OF JESUS CHRIST

THE LORDSHIP OF JESUS CHRIST - THE FOUNDATION

The Church, the Body of Christ, is built upon the foundation of the Lordship of Jesus Christ. Our life is not our own. It belongs to Christ and we obey Him as Lord of our lives. *"Simon Peter answered, '**You are the Christ, the Son of the living God**.' Jesus replied, 'Blessed are you Simon son of Jonah, for this was not revealed to you by man, but by my Father in heaven. And I tell you that you are Peter, and on this rock (i.e. that Jesus Christ is Lord) I will build my church, and the gates of Hades will not overcome it. I will give you the keys of the kingdom of heaven; whatever you bind on earth will be bound in heaven, and whatever you loose on earth will be loosed in heaven.'"* Matthew 16:16-20.

Jesus spoke of building our house upon a rock foundation in Matthew 7: 24-27. This foundation represents the Lord Himself and His truths that promise inner transformation. The sand in that parable speaks of pharisaic external and legalistic self-righteousness that can neither please God nor withstand the challenges of life (vs. 26-27).[5]

Christians do well to remember Christ's words in Matthew 7: 21-23, *"Not everyone who says to Me, 'Lord, Lord,' shall enter the kingdom of heaven, but he who does the will of My Father in heaven. Many will say to Me in that day, 'Lord, Lord, have we not prophesied in Your name, cast out demons in Your name, and done many wonders in Your name?' And then I will declare to them, 'I never knew you; depart from Me, you who practice lawlessness!'"*

THE RESULTS THAT COME FROM MAKING JESUS LORD OF OUR LIVES…

Life on our own terms is over. We are obedient to His Word. Good works come as our response to His love for us – and that's how we measure our faith (i.e. by our labor for Him). We develop relationships in the Body based upon a loving commitment to meet each other's needs. In addition, we move from isolation into a shared life.

Once the foundation is established, we can then begin building the house of God – the church. The church's BELIEFS, VALUES, and ATTITUDES come from the Word of God; and its SERVICES proceed from the ministry of the Holy Spirit.

BELIEFS AND ATTITUDES. WHAT IS ACCEPTED PRACTICE IN THE CHURCH? WHAT IS NOT ACCEPTED?

Everybody is accepted as somebody special in the church! We are ambassadors of Christ! Everyone is accepted as they are while our

---

[5] OUR DAILY BREAD, November 12, 2006, RBC Ministries.

Lord shapes us into what He wants us to become. Since we are being transformed into His image, church members are asked to receive from the ministries of the church and its leadership what is needed for that growth. Members are asked to practice those things that will cause this transformation to take place. Therefore, if there is something that needs to be corrected in our life, it may be necessary for church leaders to offer us some loving advice.

Being a member of the Body means following the leaders God gives us <u>as they follow Christ</u> (Ephesians 4:11). The church is governed by God ruling through His designated, delegated authority. This authority, however, emanates from relationship. The success of a leader depends very much upon his ability to love, care, and relate to his people. The leaders God gives us can only exercise authority as people voluntarily submit (1Thessalonians 5:12-13). Submission is always voluntary

Disagreements are to be expected in a church family. They don't happen to hurt or offend anybody, but rather as an opportunity for both people to grow and be shaped into the image of Christ. The best way to keep disputes to a minimum is as follows…

We should be open and honest in relationships rather than burying true feelings. When Christians express those feelings, however, they should do it with the love of the Lord. We need to remember His love for us in that while we were still sinners, He died for us (Romans 5:8). We also should keep our lives connected to Christ through the spiritual vitamins of Chapter 4. And the church services and ministries help us do that. Christians should also commit themselves to embracing Christ's values given in Chapter 1 in order to put on "the mind of Christ" and emulate Him. Finally, disputes will be minimized by Church leaders emphasizing to members that we must stay ready to meet the Lord at any time.

SINNING IS SERIOUS EVEN FOR CHRISTIANS

We must stay ready to meet the Lord. Jesus said, *"So you must keep watch because you do not know when the owner of the house will come back – whether in the evening, or at midnight, or when the rooster crows, or at dawn. If he comes suddenly, don't let him find you sleeping. What I say to you, I say to everyone: 'Watch'"* Mark 13: 35-37. Also see Luke 12:35-40.

What's most important is the attitude of the heart towards sinning. The real issue is how deeply we sense the implications of our sins. Are we filled with godly sorrow? Are we pained by the tragic consequences our sin creates in our relationships with others? We don't mean a phony show of sorrow. Do we feel some of the same sorrow God feels about evil? Are we willing to turn from it?

WHAT IS EXPECTED OF ME IN TERMS OF PRACTICAL CHRISTIANITY IN RELATION TO OTHER CHURCH MEMBERS AND ALSO THOSE OUTSIDE THE CHURCH?

The life of a Christian is a shared life. We are expected to help one another in both spiritual and material ways when God leads us. See Acts 2:42-46. Galatians 5:13 says, *"You, my brothers, were called to be free. But do not use your freedom to indulge your sinful nature; rather, serve one another in love."*

TITHING. Giving 10% of our gross income to the church for paying its bills is consistent with the Bible. Malachi 3:8-10 asks the question, *"Will a man rob God?"* It then explains that all the tithes should be brought into God's "storehouse", that there might be "meat" in God's house. Romans 12:13 tells us to share with people who are in need – to practice hospitality. Galatians 6:6 tells us to share good things with those who instruct us in God's Word.

WITNESSING TO NON-CHRISTIANS – WHAT'S THE BEST WAY TO WITNESS? We should always be ready to share our testimony with non-believers. It should be done with grace and seasoned with "salt". The best way the church can witness to our community is by being one in heart and soul with the people of our congregation. See John 17:21.

WHAT'S EXPECTED OF ME IN RELATING TO CHRISTIANS OUTSIDE MY LOCAL CHURCH AND IN THEIR PROGRAMS AND EVENTS? Participating in other Christian ministries is an accepted practice. It should be understood, however, that our primary place to serve is where the Lord has planted us. We draw others to our church through guest speakers, door-to-door handouts, mailings, radio and other media ads. Follow-up is always essential.

WHAT IS ACCEPTED PRACTICE WHEN IT COMES TO DRAWING OTHERS TO OUR CHURCH – CHRISTIANS AND NON-CHRISTIANS? There are already too many Christians who leave their own church to find the "perfect" church. So we should not encourage other Christians to leave their present church. Christians who have no church and are searching should be invited. Non-Christians are always welcome in our services.

HOW DOES THE CHURCH HELP ME TO GROW IN CHRIST? HOW DO I HELP OTHERS GROW IN CHRIST? We help members grow in Christ by providing many opportunities to learn the Word and to practice the Word through service to others. We also provide times of worship, fellowship, prayer, and times of comfort. The members, however, are never forced to attend. They need to voluntarily take advantage of these times.

HOW DO I REALIZE THE SPIRITUAL GIFTS I HAVE? There are courses available to help you find the most probable area of ministry. However, the church leadership can help to give you confirmation of a gift.

HOW DOES THE CHURCH ENCOURAGE ME TO USE MY GIFT TO BENEFIT OTHERS? The leaders will invite you to participate in various ministries depending upon your gifts.

ARE THERE GUIDELINES FOR ME ABOUT SPIRITUAL GIFTS? See Chapter 16.

HOW DO I BECOME A MEMBER OF THE CHURCH? Many churches have a course which they offer to prospective members which covers in depth the material in this brief church guide.

HOW DOES THE CHURCH MEASURE SUCCESS? The church Board should spend time at their meetings discussing these measures and especially how to move the church to higher levels. Some of the input can come from church members themselves through a periodic survey by the Board. Here are some measures that should be considered…

SUNDAY SCHOOL ATTENDANCE – The number of people attending both the adult and children classes.

NUMBER OF NEW BELIEVERS COMING TO CHRIST THROUGH CHURCH SERVICES – Sunday morning, men's and women's ministries, Boys and Girls Christian Service programs, etc.

NUMBER OF CHURCH MEMBERS READING THE BIBLE THROUGH IN A YEAR

PERCENT OF CHURCH MEMBERS WHO STUDY THE WORD IN A PRIVATE TIME WITH THE LORD

PERCENT OF CHURCH MEMBERS WHO HAVE A PRIVATE DAILY PRAYER TIME

NUMBER OF SANCTIONED (BY THE CHURCH) SMALL GROUPS MEETING REGULARLY

PERCENT OF CHURCH MEMBERS WATER-BAPTIZED

PERCENT OF CHURCH MEMBERS IN A MINISTRY SERVING OTHERS

PERCENT OF MEMBERS COMMITING TO THE "SPIRITUAL VITAMINS", "CHRIST'S VALUES AND BEHAVIORS OF CHAPTER 1.

WHAT SERVICES DOES THE CHURCH PROVIDE TO ITS MEMBERS? WHAT THINGS ARE MANDATORY VERSUS VOLUNTARY?

There are many services provided including Sunday school, Bible studies, programs for men, women, boys and girls, community outreach, small groups, social events and more. The only mandatory services are as follows…

WATER BAPTISM – mandatory but Christians must do this voluntarily. It is mandatory because Jesus said in the Great Commission, *"Therefore go and make disciples of all nations, baptizing them in the name of the Father, Son, and Holy Spirit, and teaching…"* Matthew 28:19. Also see Acts 8:16; 19:5; Romans 6:3; 1 Corinthians 1:13; 10:2; Galatians 3:27.

COMMUNION – mandatory. This is mandatory because at the Last Supper, *"He took some bread, gave thanks and broke it, and gave it to them, saying, 'This is my body given for you; do this in remembrance of me.'"* Luke 22:19. See also 1Corinthians 11:17-34. When believers observe this ordinance, we should take spiritual inventory and reflect on the huge cost of our redemption. This is our opportunity to confess our sins and receive forgiveness. When we confess our sins, the Lord is faithful and just to forgive our sins and cleanse us from all unrighteousness (1John 1:9). So then, everyone can receive these emblems of the Lord's broken Body and Blood.

SUNDAY & MIDWEEK WORSHIP SERVICES – mandatory but voluntary. This is mandatory because we read, *"And let us consider how we may spur one another on toward love and good deeds. Let us not give up meeting together, as some are in the habit of doing, but let us encourage one another – and all the more as we see the Day approaching."* Hebrews 10:24-25.

CHAPTER 14 - Warning!! Some Churches Act Like Cults

"Watch out for false prophets. They come to you in sheep's clothing, but inwardly they are ferocious wolves. By their fruit you will recognize them. Do people pick grapes from thornbushes, or figs from thistles? Likewise every good tree bears good fruit, but a bad tree bears bad fruit." (Matthew 7: 15-16).

There are many movements and independent churches that practice abusive styles of discipleship and leadership. They are genuinely Christian groups because their fundamental doctrines agree with historic Christianity. They add to these teachings, however, secondary doctrines and practices that the Church down through the centuries has not endorsed.

Some say that they are the only churches or groups practicing "real Christianity." One of these practices is to control almost every area of a member's life – to gain total loyalty and commitment. These groups are so close to the truth, and the error is so subtle, that someone trying to get a grasp on the problems over time often finds himself "losing his grip."

Here are the seven ways that Satan ambushes and deceives whole communities of believers and entraps them in error...[6]

---

[6] Adapted from ***The Dark Side of Discipleship*** by Lawrence A. Pile.

MISINTERPRETING SCRIPTURE

This is the basic reason for discipleship abuse. The other attributes presented later all come from this one. Being careless in reading and interpreting Scripture leads to dangerous teachings and erroneous conclusions in otherwise good churches. This is a trick of Satan that he used against Christ in the wilderness, *"If you are the Son of God,"* he said, *"throw yourself down from here* (i.e. the highest point of the temple in Jerusalem). *For it is written, 'He will command his angels concerning you to guard you carefully; and they will lift you up in their hands, so that you will not strike your foot against a stone.'"* The devil was quoting from Psalm 91:11-12. Christ corrected this misinterpretation – that we could be reckless and endanger ourselves to test God – by giving the greater truth which is, *"Do not put the Lord your God to the test."* (Deuteronomy 6:16).

Failure to read the Bible carefully and use the proper principles of interpretation (i.e. historical, cultural, and textual context) can result in ideas that the Holy Spirit never intended (e.g. communal living). Satan ambushes Christians by causing churches to confuse biblical examples with actual commands. These churches insist that because Paul or other persons in the Bible did something or lived a certain way, then every believer should do likewise. Sometimes they take their own common practices and raise them up to the status of a biblical command.

General principles like *"...not giving the devil a foothold"* (Ephesians 4:27) are used by unscriptural autocratic leaders to determine what activities, places, and attitudes are wrong for their people. Unless the Word of God, however, specifically agrees with their opinions, these interpretations are not binding on anyone. Every believer needs to learn how to go to God directly in prayer and how to study the Scriptures to seek the Lord's guidance. Also, a church leader does not have the authority to legislate direction in areas where the Bible is silent.

AUTOCRATIC LEADERSHIP

Groups and churches that abuse discipleship expect and often demand almost total submission of members with little or no ability to question a leader's teaching or actions. Though there are many times when it is wise to seek advice from leaders, in these groups advice is given as a command whether requested or not – even in very small matters. People in these groups become so dependent upon getting this guidance that they have trouble making the simplest decisions – what color curtains to choose or what store to shop in. Refusing to submit in even the smallest of matters causes a sincere Christian to be labeled as a rebel and agitator.

These churches lack the balance of Scripture concerning leadership. They might ascribe to Hebrews 13:17, *"Obey your leaders and submit to their authority."* However, 1 Peter 5:2-3 is not followed, *"Be shepherds of God's flock that is under your care...not lording it over those entrusted to you, but being examples to the flock."* Leaders are to seek God *with* their people – not *for* their people. The destructive consequence of this autocratic leadership is that believers are deprived of their right and responsibility to seek God for themselves. The guidance of the Holy Spirit, promised by Christ to lead us into all truth, is dismissed and church members are left with an unchallenged acceptance of their leader's opinions and decisions.

ISOLATIONISM

Groups or churches that abuse discipleship assert that they are "protecting their people" by isolating them from harmful influences." Members are usually discouraged from listening to any Bible teachers except those from their own church. They are told that if these other teachers knew the truth, they would belong to their church. As for relationships with the opposite sex, these groups usually strongly discourage dating. Instead there's a match-making that's done by leaders – "by divine guidance".

Permission from the leaders is essential for marriage and the other partner must come from a member of their own church.

SPIRITUAL ELITISM

As we have indicated above, groups or churches that abuse discipleship think that nobody else is following the New Testament as closely as they are. Ronald Enroth quotes an ex-member of one of these groups as saying, "Although we didn't come right out and say it, in our innermost hearts we really felt that there was no place in the world like our assembly...We thought the rest of Christianity was out to lunch."[7] There's also an attempt by these churches to provide a total package for their members of everything needed so they will not go outside their group to get "second-best" sources. So some groups will publish their own newspapers, magazines, devotionals, recording companies, home-school institutes, or even investment firms. Sometimes they purchase their own radio stations. The intent is to exert pressure to believe in their parochial views.

REGIMENTATION OF LIFE

Under the guise of making disciples, these churches and groups have rules to live by that go way beyond what most evangelicals would condone. These include rules about morality, ethics, and values. Those who are professionals and who have studied these organizations conclude that members are not being shaped into the image of Christ. Instead, they are shaped into the image of their leaders.

Members seem to think that their continued progress in holiness as Christians depends upon their own efforts – on the flesh (See Galatians 3:3). The Apostle Paul has said about righteousness that it *"is by faith first to last."* (Romans 1:17). He also said, *"It is for freedom that Christ has set us free. Stand firm, then, and do not let*

---

[7] *Voices From The Fringe*, Moody Monthly, October 1989

yourselves be burdened again by a yoke of slavery." (Galatians 5:1).

DISALLOWANCE OF DISSENT

Members are expected to bury any objections or questions. This is reinforced by repeated teachings on the importance of "unity." What is actually taught is not singleness of purpose and being "one in the Spirit" (See Philippians 2:2), but rather uniformity in all matters, where other churches allow a wide latitude.

In most of these groups and churches that abuse discipleship, denying dissent extends to anything that might be perceived as undermining the authority of the leaders. Even when trying to correct the leader privately for minor mistakes with history, the church member might be accused of insubordination. When the group's basic teachings are questioned, the member is accused of not being submissive – and if his heart were right, he'd understand.

TRAUMATIC DEPARTURE

Anyone who continues to question or dissent experiences a painful confrontation with leaders. Ex-members have called this a "surprise party" or "gang-up." This is usually un-announced, has 4 or 5 leaders to one dissident, runs for hours, with the purpose of showing the church member his error. Occasionally, the member will have the courage to withstand such a confrontation and continue to insist that his leader take his concerns seriously. Ultimately, this ends in total excommunication. The group member finds himself cut-off from former friends – the leaders usually tell their group that the dissident is "off-limits." In some cases ex-members have found it necessary to change jobs because they no longer felt comfortable working with (or for) members of the group.

In addition, marriages can break apart by one partner remaining faithful to the group. There are nervous breakdowns and suicides of members who can't cope any longer with the church or group but are unable to find a way out.

CONCLUSION

It should be obvious to every sincere Christian that no fellowship should ever allow Satan to create such an atmosphere in the Church that would lead anyone of its members to consider running away from God in order to relieve the pressure. However, in their earnest and sincere efforts to obey the Great Commission, some Christian leaders have been deceived into using methods to speed spiritual growth that are not biblical and are very dangerous.

CHAPTER 15 - Guide To Christian Ethics

How Do Christians Decide What Is Right Or Wrong?[8]

How do Christians decide what is right and what is wrong? Morality for Christians is living God's way. Christian morality is not based on a set of rules or laws.

God's Word, the Bible, is all sufficient for giving us instructions on how to live the Christian life. It provides detailed instructions on what to do in various situations in our lives. It also describes God's nature, character qualities and priorities, as well as His actions that are all prompted by unselfish love. We know, however, that the Bible does not <u>explicitly</u> cover every single situation we will face in our lives. How then is it sufficient? That is where **Christian ethics** enters the picture.

SEARCH FOR THE PRINCIPLE

While God's Word does not cover each and every situation we will face in our lives, it is all sufficient for living a Christian life. Most

---

[8] Adapted from www.gotquestions.org, Wycliffe Dictionary of Christian Ethics by Carl Henry, and www.request.org.uk .

things we can simply see what the Bible says and follow the proper course based on that. In the cases where Scripture does not give explicit instructions for a given situation, we need to look for the principle behind it. In many of those cases it will be easy if a Christian knows God's Word.

Most of the principles Christians follow are sufficient for most situations. In the rare case, where there is neither explicit Scripture, nor seemingly a clear principle, we need to rely on God. **We must study His Word to know His will and pray over His Word. The Holy Spirit will teach us and guide us through the Bible to find the principle we need to stand on so we may walk and live as a Christian should.**

CONSIDER BASIC CHRISTIAN BELIEFS.

When trying to decide what is the right thing to do, Christians look to their basic beliefs for guidelines. The Bible was written many years ago and topics such as contraception, euthanasia, genetic research, and many other issues are not explicitly discussed, but the basic beliefs outlined in the Bible can act as guidelines helping Christians to come to moral decisions and to work out what they believe God wants them to do. For example, when considering how we should treat others, animals or our environment, a Christian needs to bear in mind the basic belief that God created the world and made humans custodians of this earth.

Christian ethics involves finding the principles, derived from the Word of God, by which we act. While God's Word may not cover each and every situation we face throughout our lives, its principles give us the standards by which we must carry ourselves in those situations where there are no explicit instructions. For example the Bible does not say anything explicitly on the use of illegal drugs, yet based on the principles we learn through Scripture we can know that it is wrong.

We know it's wrong because the Word of God tells us that our body is a temple of the Holy Spirit and that we should honor God with it (1 Corinthians 6:19-20). Knowing what these drugs do to our body, the harm they cause to various organs, we know that by using them we would be destroying the temple of the Holy Spirit. That is certainly not honoring to God. We also know that using illegal drugs is wrong because the Bible also tells us that we are to follow the authorities that God Himself has put into place (Romans 13:1). Given the illegal nature of the drugs today, by using them, you are not submitting to the authorities, but rather, rebelling against them.

SEARCH DEEPER AND CONSIDER THE GREATEST COMMANDMENTS.

By using the principles we find in Scripture, Christians can determine their course for any given situation. In some cases it will be simple, like the discussion of Christian living in Colossians chapter 3. That chapter begins, *"Since, then, you have been raised with Christ, set your hearts on things above, where Christ is seated at the right hand of God. Set your minds on things above, not on earthly things. For you died and your life is now hidden with Christ in God. When Christ, who is your life, appears, then you also will appear with him in glory. Put to death, therefore, whatever belongs to your earthly nature: sexual immorality, impurity, lust, evil desires and greed, which is idolatry. Because of these, the wrath of God is coming"* (Colossians 3:1-6).

In other cases, however, we need to search deeper. Christians make moral decisions by trying to work out what God would want them to do.

As a rule, Christians should always be trying to obey the commandments that Jesus called the two greatest - to love God FIRST and to love other people. What is moral, then, is whatever demonstrates our love for God FIRST and then whatever demonstrates our love to others.

Those two commandments are given in Mark 12: 28-31, *"One of the teachers of the law came and heard them debating. Noticing that Jesus had given them a good answer, he asked him 'Of all the commandments, which is the most important?' 'The most important one,' Jesus answered, 'is this: Hear, O Israel, the Lord our God, the Lord is one. Love the Lord your God with all your heart, with all your soul and with all your mind and with all your strength. The second is this: Love your neighbor as yourself. There is no commandment greater than these.'"*

KEEP A VIBRANT LIVING RELATIONSHIP WITH GOD THROUGH CHRIST.

Christians believe that the Bible is God's revelation of Himself to the world. They look to the Bible to find out what God might have to teach about any particular issue. Christians consider studying the Bible to be very important, because it contains details of how God wants them to live. Although subjects such as abortion and use of genetic research might not be explicitly addressed in the Bible, Christians believe that the Bible has much to say on these modern issues because many of the guiding principles contained in the Bible are relevant to these issues (such as where life comes from, the importance of justice, mercy and forgiveness, and the sanctity of life).

Study of God's Word is inextricably connected to <u>relationship with God</u>. Other spiritual disciplines also help to strengthen that relationship. For example, our Lord will confirm what you read in His Word while you pray or worship Him. He may also speak through a close friend or while you are ministering to confirm His Word.

Therefore, the best way to determine what is right or wrong, in my opinion, is to maintain a vibrant, living relationship with God through daily study of His Word, continuous prayer for knowing what to do in all situations and moral issues, fellowshipping with God's people, worshipping Him daily, and serving Him in a ministry. The Holy Spirit indwells each and

every believer, and He is faithful in using our living relationship with the Lord (especially God's Word and prayer) to teach us how to live:

"But the Counselor, the Holy Spirit, whom the Father will send in my name, will teach you all things and will remind you of everything I have said to you." (John 14:26). *"As for you, the anointing you received from him remains in you, and you do not need anyone to teach you. But as his anointing teaches you about all things and as that anointing is real, not counterfeit—just as it has taught you, remain in him."* (1 John 2:27).

So when we pray over Scripture, fellowship with faithful, caring Christians, worship and serve the Lord, the Spirit will guide us and teach us. He will show us the principle we need to stand on for any given situation.

"It was he (i.e. Christ) who gave some to be apostles, some to be prophets, some to be evangelists, and some to be pastors and teachers, to prepare people for works of service, so that the body of Christ may be built up until we reach unity in the faith and in the knowledge of the Son of God and become mature, attaining the full measure of perfection found in Christ."

- Ephesians 4:11-13

"Therefore go and make disciples of all nations, baptizing them in the name of the Father and of the Son and of the Holy Spirit, and teaching them to obey everything I have commanded you."

Jesus – Matthew 28: 19-20

CHAPTER 16 - Guide To Spiritual Gifts And A Roadmap To Salvation

Our Lord has given every Christian the gifts He wants them to use for the benefit of the Body of Christ. We are channels that the Lord works through to minister to others. Many of these spiritual gifts are identified in Romans 12, 1 Corinthians 12, and Ephesians 4. Here's a list and explanation of what appears in these chapters...

GIFTS OF THE SPIRIT - WHAT ARE THEY?[9]

Gifts of the Spirit are special abilities provided by the Holy Spirit to Christians for the purpose of building up the body of Christ. The list of spiritual gifts in 1 Corinthians 12:8-10 includes **wisdom**, **knowledge**, **faith**, **healing**, **miracles**, **prophecy**, **discerning of spirits**, **speaking in tongues**, and **interpretation of tongues**. Similar lists appear in Ephesians 4:7-13 and Romans 12:3-8. These are the additional gifts mentioned there: **helping**, **administration**, **teaching**, **exhortation**, **giving**, **leadership**, **showing mercy (i.e.**

---

[9] Adapted from All About God, www.allaboutgod.com, Young's Compact Bible Dictionary, 1984, Tyndale House Publishers, and My Spiritual Journey, www.umc.org.

compassion), apostleship, evangelism, shepherding (i.e. pasturing), and servanthood. The gifts of the Spirit are simply God enabling believers to do what He has called us to do. 2 Peter 1:3 says, *"His divine power has given us <u>everything we need</u> for life and godliness through our knowledge of him who called us by his own glory and goodness."* The gifts of the Holy Spirit are part of the "everything we need" to fulfill His purposes for our lives.

GIFTS OF THE SPIRIT - THE DEFINITIONS

There is some controversy as to the precise nature of each of the gifts of the Spirit, but here is a list of spiritual gifts and their basic definitions.

- The gift of **wisdom** seems to be the ability to make decisions and give guidance that is according to God's will.
- The gift of **knowledge** is the ability to have an in-depth understanding of a spiritual issue or situation.
- The gift of **faith** is being able to trust God and encourage others to trust God, no matter the circumstances.
- The gift of **healing** is the miraculous ability to use God's healing power to restore a person who is sick, injured, or suffering.
- The gift of **miracles** is being able to perform signs and wonders that give authenticity to God's Word and the Gospel message.
- The gift of **prophecy** is being able to proclaim a message from God.
- The gift of **discerning spirits** is the ability to determine whether or not a message, person, or event is truly from God.
- The gift of **tongues** is a genre of prophecy when the speaker speaks prophetically, ecstatically, and miraculously in a language he has not learned to serve the needs of the Body of Christ.
- The gift of **interpreting tongues** is the ability to translate (not a literal translation and so it is called "interpreting") the tongues speaking and communicate it back to others in their own language.

- The gift of **helping** is a gift of support and behind-the-scenes effort that make groups, families, and congregations more effective. Not everyone is gifted to lead, but many are gifted to follow and handle the tasks that are so essential, but less glamorous. Helpers love to serve others, support others, and assist others in the important work of ministry and mission. Tireless in their willingness to serve, helpers are less interested in receiving thanks and recognition than in doing good, valuable work.
- The gift of **administration** allows a person to organize people and resources for greater efficiency, effectiveness, and success. Administrators have the natural ability to apply resources where they will do the greatest good. Administrators are good with details and are deeply aware of how all the parts of a group or organization work together to achieve their goals.
- The gift of **teaching** allows people to transform data and information into life changing knowledge. Teachers do not have to stand in front of a class to teach. Often gifted teachers communicate best in informal, one-on-one settings. Teachers have the uncanny knack of helping people learn effortlessly. People internalize and retain the knowledge and learning they receive from gifted teachers. Good teachers transform more than they inform.
- The gift of **exhortation** is manifest in people who offer encouragement, wise counsel, unflagging support, and empowerment. Those who exhort stay focused on helping people maximize their own potential and live from their own gifts and skills. Exhorters help people feel good about themselves, build confidence, and not grow discouraged. Often, those with the gift of exhortation make others feel good just by being present.
- The gift of **giving** is the deep commitment to provide whatever resources are needed to support God's will and plan. In addition to radical generosity, those who possess the gift of giving have the uncanny ability to discover and channel new sources of money, time, and energy to needs.

Money management skills, grant writing abilities, and the easy knack of asking for donations and cultivating donors are among common skills of gifted givers.

- The gift of **leadership** is a visionary, and forward looking gift that enables people to stay focused on where God might be leading us as individuals, congregations, and communities at any given time. Leaders look more to where we are going rather than where we currently are, or where we have been. Leaders motivate others to work together in ways that help them achieve more together than any could on their own. Leaders provide examples of how we should order our lives to honor and glorify God.

- The gift of **compassion** (i.e. showing mercy) moves people to action on behalf of those in need. Compassion is not a simple caring about others, but such a radical caring that we have no choice but to make sacrifices for others. Those with the gift of compassion rarely ask "Should I help," but instead focus on how to help. Compassion makes us fundamentally aware of the Christ in others and springs from our desire to care for all of God's creatures and creation.

- The gift of **apostleship** compels people to reach out to new and unfamiliar groups and individuals to invite them into relationship with God and community. Apostles share the story of faith in other lands, cultures, and traditions, as well as welcoming the stranger in their own land. Apostles extend the hand of friendship to those of other generations, nations, and languages. Many apostles desire to be missionaries.

- The gift of **evangelism** is the gift of faith-sharing and proclaiming the gospel of Jesus Christ to those we meet. Evangelism is primarily a one-to-one or small group experience, grounded in building relationships with others and inviting them to make a decision for Christ. Gifted evangelists do not force their faith on others, but offer relationship with God as a gift, and are ready to tell the story of God and Christ in their own lives.

- The gift of **shepherding** is the gift of mentoring and providing spiritual guidance to others to help them mature in discipleship and faith. Shepherds take an active and individualized interest in the life of faith of others. Shepherds share from their own faith journey to make the way easier for others. Shepherds are good at asking provocative questions, recommending appropriate resources and experiences, and helping people find their own way to the next level of their development.
- The gift of **servanthood** is the gift of doing for others, sometimes to the exclusion of meeting personal needs. Servants look for ways to do for others both within and beyond the congregation and community. Servants do not choose to serve, but serve from a sense of identity and call. Gifted servants never feel put-upon or taken advantage of, but see each opportunity to do for others as a way to be true to self.

LEADING OTHERS TO BE SAVED

Though Christians will have various spiritual gifts to use for the benefit of others, there is one thing we are **ALL** called to do. We ALL are to lead others to Christ by using our <u>Godly living</u> (Galatians 5: 16-26), <u>our testimonies</u> of how we ourselves came to Christ (Revelation 12:11), <u>our unity</u> in Christ (John 17:21), and the <u>Scriptures</u> (Romans 10:17).

Historical data shows that over 75% of all conversions to Christ occur in the context of a family or personal friendship.[10] This suggests that personal evangelism (sometimes called "friendship evangelism") is the most effective method of evangelism for inviting people into a personal relationship with Christ.

Thank God, that He is Light and there is no darkness in Him. His Word is a lamp unto our feet and a light unto our path. Thank

---

[10] See Church Growth, Inc.

God, that He desires that no one should perish and that everyone should come to know the Truth. (John 3:16). He doesn't want anyone to remain wandering in a cloud of darkness. He has provided a way for every man, woman, and child to come out of the darkness and come into the true light of life. Jesus said, *"I am come that they might have life, and that they might have it more abundantly."* (John 10:10 KJV).

GODLY LIVING

The most effective way to lead people to Christ is by loving and befriending them, and living your life God's way before them. As you emulate Christ, and people see the way you handle various situations, you will help them see the difference that Christ makes. They will be drawn to ask WHY you love them as you do, and HOW you are able to deal with problems as you do. Remember the sacrifices of the Apostle Paul to win men to Christ: *"Though I am free and belong to no man, I make myself a slave to everyone, to win as many as possible...I have become all things to all men so that by all possible means I might save some. I do all this for the sake of the gospel that I may share in its blessings."* (1Corinthians 9:19-23).

Let the Lord produce the fruit of the Spirit is your life: *"But the fruit of the Spirit is love, joy, peace, patience, kindness, goodness, faithfulness, gentleness and self-control."* (Galatians 5: 22). They are all powerful soul-winning attributes!

OUR TESIMONIES

Some people you want to reach for Christ get argumentative if you rush to give them Scripture. However, no one can argue with what happened in YOUR life. You are the sole authority about that. Revelation 12:11 tells us, *"They overcame him (i.e. Satan) by the blood of the Lamb and by the word of their testimony; they did not love their lives so much as to shrink from death."*

Whenever the Lord makes a way for us to tell others about how we received Jesus as our Lord and Savior, and how He changed our lives, we must be faithful to speak and not shrink from the opportunity. There is something about your testimony that will speak volumes to your listeners.

OUR UNITY

Satan has a game plan for Christians. I believe it is spelled out in Galatians 5:15, *"If you keep on biting and devouring each other, watch out or you will be destroyed by each other."* It is sad, but true that much of the persecution in the Christian life comes from within the Church. In Zechariah 13:6 KJV, when the Lord returns and the kingdoms of this world become the kingdom of our Lord and His Christ (Revelation 11:15), the Jews will look upon the wounds of Christ, *"And one shall say unto him, 'What are these wounds in thine hands?' Then he shall answer, 'Those with which I was wounded in the house of my friends.'"*

That's because the unity of Christians is a powerful evangelistic force. Jesus said in speaking to His Heavenly Father, *"...that all of them (i.e. disciples) may be one, Father, just as you are in me and I am in you. May they be one in us so that the world may believe that you sent me."* (John 17:21).

So resist the temptation to strike back at these people when you find them in the church: Evy Envy, Rep Torn, Roscoe Macho, Aaron Arrogance, Sensitive Samantha, Grey Betray, Angela Angry, Tammy Taker, Giddy Gossip, Dizzy Disrespect, Reba Rebel, Wane Worth, Pastor Patronize, Pastor Pushy, Pastor Compete, and Pastor Mule Driver. Also be careful that you don't become one of these!

THE SCRIPTURES

Remember that *"...faith comes from hearing the message, and the message is heard through the word of Christ..."* (Romans 10:17).

Always be prepared to share Scripture with those who are seeking truth.

Here's a roadmap for leading others to Christ by having them accept by faith the following truths. These scriptures together are called the **Romans Road** because they all come from the Book of Romans. Other scriptures are also presented to supplement those from Romans…

- *"There is none righteous, no, not one."* (Romans 3:10 KJV). *"All we like sheep have gone astray; we have turned every one to his own way…"* (Isaiah 53:6 KJV). All our righteousness (i.e. "right living") is as filthy rags to God, who is pure holiness. (Isaiah 64:6)

- *"For all have sinned and come short of the glory of God."* (Romans 3:23 KJV) *"Your iniquities (i.e. sins) have separated between you and your God, and your sins have hid his face from you…"* (Isaiah 59:2 KJV) *"Wherefore, as by one man (i.e. Adam) sin entered into the world, and death by sin; and so death passed upon all men, for that all have sinned."* (Romans 5:12 KJV)

But, there is a solution…

- *"But God commends his love toward us, in that, while we were yet sinners Christ died for us."* (Romans 5:8 KJV). *"For there is one God, and one mediator between God and men, the man Christ Jesus; who gave himself a ransom for all…"* (1Timothy 2:5-6)

- *"For the wages of sin is death, but the gift of God is eternal life through Jesus Christ our Lord."* (Romans 6:23). *"Ye were… redeemed with the precious blood of Christ, as of a lamb without blemish and without spot."* (1Peter 1:18-19 KJV)

- *"For whosoever shall call upon the name of the Lord shall be saved."* (Romans 10:13 KJV)

- *"If thou shalt confess with thy mouth the Lord Jesus and shalt believe in thine heart that God hath raised him from the dead, thou shalt be saved."* (Romans10:9 KJV). *"For with the heart man believeth unto righteousness; and with the mouth confession is made unto salvation... Whosoever believeth on him shall not be ashamed."* (Romans 10: 10-11 KJV)

When we accept these truths and sincerely ask Jesus to be our Savior and Lord, we are "receiving Jesus" and are "born-again"- literally "born from above". John 1: 10-13 says that Jesus came unto his own and his own received him not. But to all those who received him, he gave them the power to become children of God – even those who believe in His name – who were born not of blood, nor the will of man, but born of God (i.e. born from above or born-again). We enter the family of God and (just like blood is common in earthly family members) God sends His Holy Spirit to take up residence in all believers (i.e. members of God's spiritual family).

There was a man of the Pharisee sect that came to Jesus at night named Nicodemas. He was a ruler of the Jews. He told Jesus that they knew He was a teacher sent from God. No one could do the miracles Jesus had done, Nicodemus said, unless God was with Him. This man was receiving/accepting Jesus only as a teacher but not for who He really was. So Jesus said unto him, *"Verily, verily, I say unto thee, Except a man be born again, he cannot see the kingdom of God."* (John 3:3 KJV)

When we are "born-again", we are "saved" from the spiritual death sentence that God has imposed on those who sin, which includes everyone: *"For the wages of sin is death, but the gift of God is eternal life through Jesus Christ our Lord"*. (Romans 6:23). Both the Old and New Testaments teach that there is life after death. The patriarchs, the psalmists, the prophets, all pointed to the future. In Hebrews we read that Abraham looked for *"a city...whose builder and maker is God."* (Hebrews 11:10 KJV) In 2Corinthians

5:1 KJV, Paul wrote of *"a building of God, an house not made with hands, eternal in the heavens."* In Genesis 5:24 KJV, Enoch *"walked with God: and he was not for God took him."* The Bible tells us that Elijah was taken up to heaven in a chariot of fire. (2 Kings 2:11).

The most powerful reason, however, for believing about life after death is the resurrection of Christ. It was witnessed by hundreds (1Corinthians 15:3-7). Though we sense in ourselves that life must be more than just our existence here, Jesus proved once for all that there is life after death.

The resurrection gives meaning to the cross. The death of Christ is terrible news if it ends there. But because of His resurrection, it is "good news" – called "the Gospel". It assures us that His work is finished – that Christ atoned for everyone's sins. It also assures us that His work was perfect and that God was satisfied with His sacrifice – that Jesus was the "propitiation" for our sins. God demonstrated His satisfaction and confirmed Christ's work on the cross to atone for sin by raising Him from the dead (Acts 13:32-33).

Jesus said, *"I am the resurrection, and the life: he that believeth in me though he were dead, yet shall he live: And whosoever that liveth and believeth in me shall never die."* (John 11:25-26 KJV). Salvation for you and me only requires our *repentance* of what *we* have done and our *acceptance* of what *Christ* has done for us. We *"call upon the name of the Lord."* God hears the cry of our repentant heart for forgiveness and "remembers" the work of His Son on our behalf. Our name is then written in heaven in the Lamb's book of *life*. (Luke 10:20; Revelation 21:27)

There was a missionary who was translating the Bible into a foreign language. He was struggling over the word for "believe". One day a *runner* brought a message to the missionary's camp. He was totally exhausted, found a hammock nearby and collapsed into it. He uttered a phrase that expressed simultaneously his weariness and his contentment at finding a delightful place to relax. They were words that the missionary had never heard before so he asked one of the natives to explain them. It turned out that the runner was saying that he was at the end of himself and was therefore resting all his weight in the hammock. The missionary then realized that these words correctly described what it meant to believe.

To believe accurately means that we must first admit that we are sinners and can't help save ourselves – we're at the end of ourselves. Then we must turn from our sin and cast ourselves totally   and   unreservedly   on   Christ   for   salvation.

"Again, if the trumpet does not sound a clear call, who will get ready for battle? So it is with you. Unless you speak intelligible words with your tongue, how will anyone know what you are saying?...If then I do not grasp the meaning of what someone is saying, I am a foreigner to the speaker, and he is a foreigner to me."

- 1Corinthians 14:8-11

GLOSSARY

LEARNING THE LINGO USED IN CHRISTIAN CIRCLES

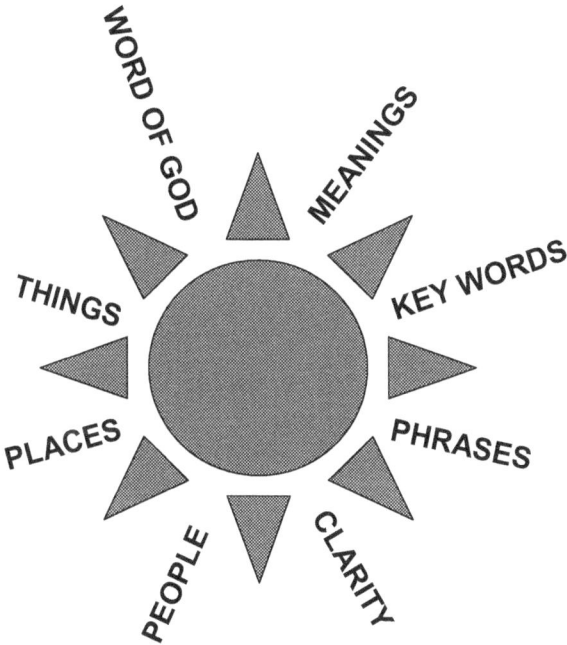

WORD OF GOD

MEANINGS

KEY WORDS

THINGS

PLACES

PHRASES

PEOPLE

CLARITY

These are some of the words and phrases Christians should be able to explain to help themselves and others get around in Christian circles...[11]

Acts, Book of – Acts is the logical sequence (part two) to the Gospel narratives, and was written by Luke, the author of the third Gospel.

Altar – A place for making sacrifices to God or pagan deities. An altar for God had to be built from earth or from unhewn stone and could not be so high that it required steps to reach its top (Exodus 20: 24-26).

Amen – Transliteration of a Hebrew word expressing agreement, similar to the English "so be it" (Numbers 5: 19-22).

---

[11] Adapted from Young's Compact Bible Dictionary, 1989, Tyndale House Publishers

Amillenialism – The belief that the 1000 year rule of Christ (Revelation 20:46) is not a physical 1000-year kingdom on earth.

Apologetics – A branch of Christian theology that seeks to make a defense of the gospel against critics, and sets forth reasons to believe in the gospel.

Arms & Armor – In defense, the body was covered with a helmet, a coat of mail or breastplate, and greaves (leg armor) of bronze. A shield or buckler was carried. Offensive weapons consisted of the sword, spear or javelin, sling, bows and arrows, battering rams.

Attributes of God – His characteristics: 1. *Omnipresent* – God is everywhere present, free of limits of space and time (Isaiah 40:12ff). 2. *Omniscient* – God is all knowing – past, present, and future (Isaiah 40:13-14). 3. *Omnipotent* – God is all powerful. He can do anything he wishes to do in alignment with his character (Psalm 115:3; Jeremiah 32:27). He has the sovereign right to rule (Romans 9:19). 4. *Spiritual* – God is in essence non-material, nonphysical. He is Spirit (John 4:24). 5. *Immutable* – God never changes. God is not evolving, devolving, getting better or worse. His perfection does not change (Malachi 3:6; James 1:17). 6. *Unity* – God is indivisible. Note this does not change the fact that God is three persons. Jesus is God (John 1:1); The Holy Spirit is God (Acts 5: 3-4); and The Father is God (Ephesians 1:3). 7. *Moral Attributes* – To name a few, the Lord is compassionate, gracious, patient; holy, just, abounding in love, wise, understanding, just, faithful, holy (Exodus 34:6-7; Daniel 2:20; 1John 4:8; Revelation 4:8; Galatians 5:22).

Backslide – A nonbiblical term that describes a lessening of one's commitment to Christ.

Baptism – John's baptism emphasizes personal repentance from sin. It may also have been an initiatory rite to the believing community, but it now involves personal activity and dedication to a new life (Luke 3:3, 10-13). The church's baptism was linked with repentance and with admission to the community of the church. A mature individual recognizing the fact that he or she is a sinner, believing in Jesus Christ as Lord and Savior, and having confessed this before men, was given the rite of baptism as a sign of spiritual cleansing and purification and admission to the church.

Big-Bang Theory – A theory about how the universe as we know it came into being, with all matter concentrated in one place, superdense. As a result of an explosion, matter became spread throughout what is now the universe, which is continuing to expand. This theory, however, cannot explain the axiom that "something cannot come from nothing". Even this superdense particle could not have eternally existed.

Blasphemy – Dishonoring and reviling the name, work, or being of God by word or deed. (1Kings 21:10,13; Isaiah 52:5).

Born-Again – The term Jesus said in John 3:3. It can also be translated "born from above." It is also a theological phrase generally referring to the act of regeneration through the Holy Spirit (Titus 3:5).

Bread – A basic staple in the diet of ancient Israel. Unleavened bread was baked immediately after grinding without the use of yeast, and it was this bread that was used at Passover and during the Feast of Unleavened Bread.

Calvary – King James version for "skull" based on the Latin version in Luke 23:33. Golgotha is the anglicized version of the Aramaic and Greek word meaning "skull." It was the place of Christ's crucifixion. It was outside the city wall of Jerusalem.

Carnal – This word in many modern versions of the Bible is "fleshly," which is the opposite of spiritual, and means to walk as a mere man, not like Christ walked.

Cell Groups - Cell groups aren't simply another name for a Bible study, fellowship group or Sunday school class. They are a group of believers who have banded together for a season in life to reach the lost, minister to the hurting and each other, and discover their leadership potential. Cell groups do study the Word, but they do so in order to live out what they read and use it effectively to penetrate a dark world with the light of Jesus Christ . . . which is quite different from studying a passage each week for general knowledge. Cell groups also have lots of fun together . . . but this fellowship is specialized in that it usually exposes unbelievers to a group of fun, Jesus-loving people. In other words, cell groups even use fellowship as an evangelistic tool! Cell groups help to live out what their pastor preaches on Sunday. Cell leaders are faithful *under-shepherds* for the senior pastor and the Lord, serving in a unique capacity to serve and love. Cell groups extend ministry and evangelism to every person in a local church body. (This was adapted from The Cell Group People, www.touchusa.org).

Christ – The name by which He is most generally known is Jesus Christ. The first name means "Savior," which shows Him to be One who came in some sense to deliver His people from bondage. The other name, Christ, is really a title meaning "Anointed One" (Messiah) and came to be used in the Jewish world for the coming leader who would introduce a new era. The main idea at the time was that Messiah would come to rid His people of the Roman tyrants, but this was far from the purpose of Jesus. When the title was applied to Him, it was used in a spiritual sense of a deliverer from moral bondage. The name Jesus Christ, therefore, puts in a nutshell what Jesus came to do.

Church – A word that is used to translate the Greek *ekklesia*, which has the idea of an assembly and is thus translated in Acts 19:32. The early believers began to organize themselves in groups or churches with various officers. Thus, it is clear that the early church thought of itself as a visible organization as well as an "invisible" one – namely, a body of all those in space and time who had come to believe in Jesus Christ (1Corinthians 12:13; Colossians 1:24).

Comforter – A title of the Holy Spirit. In the New International Standard Bible, it is translated "Counselor." (John 14:16,26).

Commandments (the Ten) – The word *Dabar* in the Old Testament emphasizes law as a direct revelation from God, as in the case of the Ten Commandments: "Ten Words" in Hebrew. Throughout the history of Western civilization and Judeo-Christian ethic, the Ten Commandments (also known as the Decalogue), have been honored as the epitome of the righteous conduct God expects of humanity.

Commitment – To have no sacrifice means to have no commitment. Commitment is at the very heart of what it is to be a real man or woman. It means to see something through – not halfway – all the way. Jesus is our best example. He gave up everything for His Father and mankind till the end. We can't be perfect like Him but we have Him as our model. How we respond to commitment says a lot about our character. (This was adapted from www.christianadvice.net).

Covenant – A pact, agreement, or treaty between persons or nations, or (in the Bible) between God and man (Genesis 21:27; 1Samuel 18:3).

Creation – The Bible presents the story of creation in the first two chapters of Genesis and clearly states it as a fact in other places (Hebrews 11:3; John 1:3,10). In summary, the picture that the Bible presents is one of all matter coming into existence only through the will and word of the eternal God.

Cross – By the time of the crucifixion of Christ by the Romans, men were affixed by nailing or by tying or both to crossed beams of wood. There were four forms. Crucifixion was a painful death, which ended in heart failure accompanied by suffocation. The cross is an integral part of Christian theology, for it was on the cross by which atonement was made to God for man the sinner, and reconciliation was achieved. In Christian theology, there is no divine remission of sin without the shedding of blood by the death of a savior, and that redemption was achieved through Christ's cross.

Crown – Normally a "crown" in the NT is a victor's wreath and not a crown often pictured with royal jeweled tiaras. Before his crucifixion, Christ was mockingly crowned with a wreath of thorns by the Roman soldiers (Matthew 27:29). The Bible speaks of crowns of glory, righteousness, life, and crowns symbolic of triumph in the Christian life (2Timothy 4:8; James 1:12; 1Peter 5:4)

Dayspring – A King James Version rendering in Job 38:12 as a name for the dawn or morning. In Luke 1:78 interpreted by many versions as a title for Christ.

Dead Sea Scrolls – Manuscripts that were found in caves west of the Dead Sea in 1947 and in subsequent years. The community that produced them lived in Qumran. The place is known today as Khirbet Qumran. The manuscripts contain portions of OT books except Esther. These documents date between the third century BC and the first century AD.

Devotions – The word "devote" means to set apart – to give up exclusively to a person or purpose. In Christian circles, devotions usually refer to setting apart time to prayer, study the Word, worship, etc.

Deities – Foreign gods, some of which were introduced in Israel. For example, Ammonite and Moabite deities were Chemosh, Milcom/Molech/Moloch.

Disciple – A pupil, one who follows some doctrine or teacher. In the NT this is a specific designation of the Twelve and all the followers of Christ (believers – later called Christians).

Elder – In the NT, each Jewish community had its council of elders, the most important of which was the Sanhedrin of Jerusalem, which served as a kind of "supreme court" for all Jewry. The church, quite naturally adopted the institution which functioned in ways comparable to the Jewish Sanhedrin. The Greek word is presbuteros, out of which comes "presbytery."

Eschatology – The study of last things, such as death, resurrection, the afterlife, divine judgment, the end of the age, and the second coming of Christ.

Eternity – Refers to the endless span of time, whether before the Creation or after the end of the present age. Called "forever," it is inhabited by God Himself (Isaiah 57:15). Eternal life is mentioned many times in the NT referring to the kind of life believers in Christ receive – for their enjoyment in this life and their reward for the life to come. Other things called eternal include: God (Deuteronomy 33:27); Purpose of God (Ephesians 3:11); Dominion of God (1Timothy 6:16); the Gospel (Revelation 14:6); God's Covenant, Salvation, Redemption, Judgment (Hebrews 5:9; 6:2; 9:12; 13:20), God's Inheritance for the Believer (Hebrews 9:15); Eternal Fire and Punishment (Matthew 25:41, 46; Jude 6-7).

Evangelism – The presentation of the gospel to someone with the purpose of bringing that one to have faith in Jesus Christ.

Exegesis – Drawing out the meaning of scripture that is already there.

Expiation – Sin is both a failure to conform to the law of God and actual transgression against it; and two things are necessary to get rid of it. One is expiation and the other is propitiation. The first requires satisfaction, the covering or blotting out of sin by a sacrifice.   The second views this satisfaction as appeasing the wrath of God because of his anger against sin.   Man's sin is expiated by Christ's sacrifice on the cross, and God's wrath against sin is propitiated.

Fellowship – A NT word which means association, communion, close relationship.   To have fellowship is to have partnership, participation, a share in something.   Christians are in this association constantly (Acts 2:42).   To have fellowship is to give material goods to believers in need and to be pleasing to God (Romans 15:26; 2Corinthians 8:4; 9:13; Hebrews 13:16).

Foot Washing – A biblical custom of foot washing performed by a host to honor his guests.   Jesus washed the disciples' feet (John 13:1-17) as a symbol of humility and love.

Forgiveness – Pardon or remission usually based on one's repenting and being willing to make restitution or reparation.   It results in the parties involved being returned to their former relationship.   To restore God's favor to man after the Fall required Him to forgive man.   This in turn required the atonement provided in the death of Christ (Colossians 1:14; 2:13-14).   Man must repent of his sin and turn from it with a desire to make restitution by living a new life.

Fornication – This is a broad word that can be used for the full spectrum of sexual sins, though often understood to mean sexual intercourse outside of marriage.   It is a symbol of idolatry, harlotry against God (Matthew 15:19; Revelation 17:4; 21:8).

Gap Theory – The theory that God created the universe (Genesis 1:1); then the earth became formless and void (a time gap) (Genesis 1:2); then the earth was remade (Genesis 1:3).   In this gap, according to the theory, geological time must have developed.

Gethsemane – The word means "olive oil press."   It's the place in the Kidron Valley on the lower slopes of the Mount of Olives where Jesus prayed the evening when Judas betrayed Him (Matthew 26:36; Mark 14:32).

Glory of the Lord (Shekinah) – The word "shekinah," from the Hebrew "to dwell," is not found in the Bible.   It was used by early rabbinical writers to refer to the appearing of God to His people – as in the pillar of cloud and fire that led the Israelites in the wilderness.   For example, God spoke to Moses through the "shekinah" out of the burning bush.

God, Names of

> **El, Elohim** – Elohim is the plural of El, which is the oldest word for "God" and most often used in the OT.   It is usually joined to a further descriptive title: El Roi – God of seeing; El Shaddai – God Almighty; El Elyon – God Most High
>
> **El Shaddai** – Shaddai probably means "sovereign power".
>
> **Adonai** – The English "Lord," represents two Hebrew words, Adonai (Supreme Master) and Yahweh.
>
> **Ab** – God the Father.
>
> **The Holy Spirit** – The word "spirit" speaks of living breath.   An attribute or work of the Spirit of God is the living energy of God active in the world and among men.
>
> **Alpha and Omega** – These are the first and last letters of the Greek alphabet.   The name indicates that God is eternal: nothing comes before or after Him; therefore, all is under His control.
>
> **Messiah** – "Anointed One".   It was also applied to the great Deliverer, whom for centuries God promised to send to restore and save His people.
>
> **Son of God** – This represents the eternal Son standing in a unique relationship to God, being Himself divine.   The union of the divine and human had been ensured by His unique birth, so the angel told Mary, "So the holy one to be born will be called 'the Son of God.'" (Luke 1:35).
>
> **Son of Man** – This is the name by which Jesus most frequently referred to Himself.   In Jesus' use of it, the name was associated with His coming suffering and resurrection (Mark 8:31) and with His coming divine glory.
>
> **The Word** – The Greek word "logos," translated "Word," in John 1:14, signifies not only speech, but the context of speech, the reason and wisdom which are expressed in the uttered word.

Gospels, the Four – The four Gospels form one pillar of the historical testimony concerning the origin of Christianity.   The other pillar is the testimony of Paul, linked to the Book of Acts.

There is good reason for advocating the traditional authorship of the Gospels: two by apostles, Matthew and John; two by men closely associated with the apostles, Mark with Peter and Luke with Paul. We are thus assured of the highest degree of historic truth from eyewitness sources (Luke 1:1-4).

Grace – In the NT, "grace" means: God's free and unmerited love and favor for sinful man shown when He did enter into the covenant of grace, to deliver them out of the estate of sin and misery, and into an estate of salvation by the Redeemer, Jesus Christ. God Himself, in the person of the Son sacrificed Himself in the crucifixion, and thereby reconciled the sinner to God and made Himself propitious to that sinner. This is free grace, not earned or earnable by man (Ephesians 2: 1-22; 3:1-7). Sometimes we define it as God's Riches At Christ's Expense.

Great Commission – This refers to Christ's charge to all Christians to "…go and make disciples of all nations, baptizing them in the name of the Father and of the Son and of the Holy Spirit, and teaching them to obey everything I have commanded you." (Matthew 28:19).

Hallelujah – a Hebrew word consisting of two parts: Hallelu meaning "You all praise!" And Ya, a shortened form of the word Yahweh, the word for Lord.

Heart – In Christian circles, this means the seat of almost all the emotions: sadness and gladness, fearfulness and confidence, loving and hating, good and bad desires. It is translated in the NIV as "mind" and "idea" (Isaiah 46:8; Numbers 16:28).

Hermeneutics – From the Greek word for "interpretation", this pertains to the method used for explaining the Bible. There are usually principles set down in any hermeneutical system. The Bible has been interpreted allegorically, literally, liberally, and existentially.

Holiness - The basic concept in the words, holy, holiness, hallow, sanctify, and sanctification is a separation and uniqueness from pagan culture. In the Bible it is separation from sin and evil and separation unto God and His ways.

Hosanna – A word that literally means, "Save us please!" but which was and is used as an exclamation of praise (Matthew 21:9).

Humble – Humility has a positive sense with respect to one's not thinking too highly of one's self and his/her social standing. God pours out His favor on humble persons. Humility is a requirement for a heavenly reward (Matthew 18:4; 23:12; Luke 14:11; 18:14).

I Am (Yahweh) - Jesus Christ gave seven titles of who He was:

> John 6:35 I am the Bread of Life.
> John 8:12 I am the Light of the World.
> John 10:7 I am the Door of the sheep.
> John 10:11 I am the Good Shepherd.
> John 11:25 I am the Resurrection and the Life.
> John 14:6 I am the Way, the Truth, and the Life.
> John 15: 1 I am the true Vine.

Inerrancy – The belief that the Bible has no error (not even in history or science), normally ascribed to original documents.

Infallibility – The belief that God's Word will not fail in its purpose.

Kenosis – The Greek word meaning empty. The doctrine of kenosis applies to Christ's emptying of Himself and taking upon Himself humanity and the position of a servant. (Philippians 2:7).

Judgment – An opinion passed down by men, or as is more often the case, a sentence or an actual calamity sent by God for punishment. More notable among these are: The Fall, the Flood, the confounding of tongues at the Tower of Babel, the Babylonia captivity, the deliverance of believers by the judgment placed upon Christ, and the final judgment of those who fail to accept that deliverance worked out by Christ (Genesis 3:1ff; 11:1-8; Deuteronomy 28:15,25,58-68; Matthew 25:31ff; John 3:16-19; 2Thessalonians 1:5-10; 2Peter 3:8-13).

Kingdom of God – God's kingdom consists of all those who accept and serve Jesus Christ as Lord (or King). It is here now in the hearts of men and women and will be established literally on earth for a time before it becomes eternal (Matthew 12:28; John 3:3, 5-7; 1Corinthians 15:24-26).

Lamp, Lampstand – It's a vessel for giving light and its stand. Lampstands are usually mentioned in connection with the golden candlestick (lampstand) in the tabernacle and temple. It is only natural that the lighted lamp would have symbolic meaning, speaking to man of the light of God; His Word, His salvation, and

His guidance (Psalm 119:105; 2Peter 1:19; Isaiah 62:1; Psalm 18:28).

Law – The key word for law in the OT, "torah," means "instruction" or guidance." It usually refers to the sum total of gracious covenant relation between Yahweh and Israel.

Laying On of Hands – In both testaments this act could mean the giving of a blessing, benediction, or parental inheritance, or the bestowal of the gifts and rights of an office. In the NT it was the external symbol of the giving of the Holy Spirit to an individual (Acts 19:6). By extension, from 1Timothy 4:14 and 2Timothy 1:6, it became the procedure for the ordination of one of its leaders.

Life – It may refer to two parts of man's existence: the period of his earthly existence, his lifetime, or to his eternal existence into which he enters through death. Both are presented as gifts of God to His creatures.

Lord's Supper – The name commonly given to the meal that Jesus ate with His disciples the night before He was crucified, the supper which started as a Passover meal but which Jesus changed as a memorial service to be kept by the church until He returns (Matthew 26:17, 26-28; 1Corinthians 10:16; 11:17-32).

Love – In the NT, the main thrust is that God is love by nature, and man's chief end is to love God supremely and to glorify Him by keeping His commandments. There is emphasis also upon the need for man to love his fellowman (1John 4:7-12, 16, 19-21).

Love Feast (Agape feast) – While the term is only found once (Jude 12), the concept grew up in the early church from a communal meal apparently eaten in connection with the observance of the Lord's Supper.

Marriage – The union of a man and a woman first consummated in the Garden of Eden by Adam and Eve. This union became the pattern for all others to follow (Genesis 2:24; Matthew 19:46). The function of marriage was more than to enable two people to love and live together. It was to produce a progeny and to supervise the raising of the children to be an object lesson of the relation of God to His people. In this the role of parents is particularly important and is very clear in the OT and NT (Isaiah 54:56; Ephesians 5:21 – 6:4).

Midtribulationalism – The view that halfway through the Great Tribulation in Revelation the church will be raptured.

Mind – The translation of a number of Greek and Hebrew words which involve both the reflective thinking of the brain and the emotional thinking associated with the heart. The heart was considered the center of the entire personality and as such a natural rendering would be "mind."

New Jerusalem – It's a new holy city where God Himself will dwell with His saints (Revelation 3:12; 21:2).

Obedience – The biblical concept is a hearing that takes place and the need to comply with what is heard. Obedience is the supreme test of faith in God (1Samuel 15:22-24) or as the NT puts it, "Faith without works is dead." (James 2: 14-16).

One Another – The Greek word for one another (*allelon*) has the idea of mutuality and reciprocity. It is a beautiful and edifying concept pertaining to Christian interpersonal relationships. There are 30 "one another" scriptures in the NT. This concept relates to "fellowship."

Pastors - (those who give pasture to sheep). The pastor is the religious shepherd or leader of a people.

Pentateuch – This term literally means "five in a case." It refers to the first five books of the Bible, also known as the torah or law and commonly called "The Five Books of Moses."

Postmillennialism – A belief that in the end times Christ will return at the end of the Millennium. Those of this view see Christ reigning through His church during the Millennium and not physically or bodily.

Praise – The giving of thanks, blessing or glory especially to God (Genesis 29:35; 1Chronicles 16:4; Psalm 146:1; Luke 19:37: Ephesians 1: 6-14). Praises often take the form of poems or songs (1Chronicles 16:9; 2Chronicles 29:30).

Predestination – The word is defined in Acts 4:28 as that which God predetermined in His plan. In Romans 8: 28-29, Paul made the point that God calls according to His purposes those whom He predetermined would be conformed to the image of His Son. God predestines both events and persons, both individuals and groups. This is otherwise called His election and those affected are called the elect.

Premillennialism – The belief that Christ will come to earth for 1000 years and rule on the earth.

Pride – Pride is a character flaw according to scripture. Arrogance, loftiness, boasting (verbalized pride), haughtiness are synonyms. Often the rich are characterized as proud. The Lord will be against the proud (Proverbs 15:25; Isaiah 2:11; Amos 6:8). And pride is part of the world's system (1John 2:16).

Promise – As God does not change, His Word is His promise. Great OT promises were made to or about individuals (e.g. to those in the Garden of Eden (Genesis 3: 14-19) and to Abraham (Genesis 15:18).

Prophet, Prophecy – Two basic concepts underlie these words: forthtelling and foretelling. The first is more basic and frequent. It means that one person becomes the "mouthpiece" for another, often consoling or correcting. Aaron played this role for his brother Moses (Exodus 7:1). The foretelling means predicting things before they happen. Prior to the time of Samuel, prophets were called "seers" in Israel; and later on there were schools of prophets and those in them were called "sons of the prophets" (2Kings 4:38). There were prophets who wrote their prophecies like Jeremiah, Isaiah, and Ezekiel. But the earliest ones did not write but spoke only like Elijah and Elisha.

Propitiation - Sin is both a failure to conform to the law of God and actual transgression against it; and two things are necessary to get rid of it. One is expiation and the other is propitiation. The first requires satisfaction, the covering or blotting out of sin by a sacrifice. The second views this satisfaction as appeasing the wrath of God because of his anger against sin. Man's sin is expiated by Christ's sacrifice on the cross, and God's wrath against sin is propitiated.

Rapture – A Latin term that means "to catch up" (1Thessalonians 4:17). It is the removal of the church from earth. There are primarily four views: Midtribulational; Partial (i.e. not all the church is raptured at the same time); Posttribulational; and Pretribulational.

Redeeming the Time – KJV for "making the most of every opportunity" (Ephesians 5:16; Colossians 4:5).

Resurrection – It means rising from the dead. In the biblical concept, man in a disembodied state is incomplete. The departed soul is waiting for the redemption of the body. At the resurrection of the body the two are joined again for eternity (Romans 8:23; 2Corinthians 5:3ff). Christ's resurrection is the capstone of all his ministry and his teaching. It is by that fact that He is declared to be the Son of God with power (Romans 1:4). His resurrection was necessary to complement His atoning death (Romans 4: 24-25).

Revelation – It means the "making known of truth." God makes himself known to man (1) in nature, (2) in the person and work of His Son, and (3) by His Spirit speaking to holy men of old who recorded what was revealed to them in a historical document that became known as the Scriptures or the Bible (Psalm 19:1ff; John 14: 8-9; 2Corinthians 5:19; Colossians 1:15).

Righteousness – The basic concept in the word is rightness or justness in whatever context it is presented. Man is incapable in his own efforts to make himself righteous in God's sight; that is why the NT presents the concept of righteousness coming through the atoning work of Christ imputed to the believer.

Sabbath – The last day of a 7-day week. Following the precedent found in Creation where God finished all His work in six days and rested on the seventh, the seventh day has become for the Jews the day of rest, prayers, and worship.

Sacrament - A sacred ceremony which is regarded as a cause or a sign of grace.

Sacrifices – There were five distinct kinds of Mosaic sacrifices, each with its own special ritual. The immediate purpose of the offerings was religious symbolism. The NT specifically relates the sacrifices to Christ's redemptive work.

Saint – It means unique, consecrated, or holy one. In the NT it came to have more frequent reference to those who were "in Christ" (i.e. to Christians).

Salvation – Man is fallen, lost, and under condemnation. Salvation is the renewal and restoration of man from all he lost in the Fall. It is not only escape from God's wrath, but deliverance from all the effects of sin, including also the spiritual blessings which come in Christ. Salvation is available only by accepting Jesus Christ as Savior and following Him as Lord.

Samaritans – When the leaders of Samaria and surrounding areas were deported by the Assyrians, the leaders of other communities were brought in to replace them. The intermarriage of the people produced the Samaritans, who came to be disliked by the Jews.

Seal – An engraved stamp, ring, or cylinder for making an impression which would be proof of authenticity, either the substitute for or the authenticating of a signature. In the NT, believers are said to be sealed with the promised Holy Spirit and sealed for the day of redemption (Ephesians 1:13; 4:30).

Sects – Groups that hold to a certain philosophy considered heresy or unorthodox. Some of those groups include: Epicureans, Stoics, Gnostics, Scribes, Sadducees, Pharisees, Zealots, Essenes, Nicolaitans, Herodians, and Hellenists.

Secular – It is anything that is not religious.

Sin – The essence of sin is willful disobedience to the declared will of God. When sin entered the world, it brought in its aftermath sorrow, suffering, and death. Sin became and still remains the great curse of human life.

Spiritual Gifts – As used in the NT, these words refer to certain extraordinary gifts given to Christians by the Holy Spirit to equip them for ministry, whether preaching, or other service. Lists of them are given in Romans 12: 6-8; 1Corinthians 12: 1-11; 28-30; Ephesians 4: 7-12.

Stumbling Block – A snare set in a pathway which would cause one to fall. This word can be an enticement to sin (Revelation 2:14). It also has the idea of an obstacle or hindrance. The cross of Christ was a hindrance to the belief of the Jews (1 Corinthians 1:23).

Tabernacle – It means "tent," and was the portable shrine provided for worship of God during the period of wandering in the wilderness, while the Israelites of the Exodus were making their way to Canaan.

Temple – In the 4th year of Solomon's reign (c965B.C.), construction began on the national temple of Israel in Jerusalem (1Kings 6:1). Its dimensions were double the size of the tabernacle: 90feet long x 30feet wide x 45feet high. The second temple was erected by Zerubbabel and finally completed about

516BC after two decades of frustration and delay. It was placed on the foundations of Solomon's temple. Around 19B.C. Herod the Great undertook a major renovation and enlargement, which was completed in A.D. 64.

Temptation – An attempt to entice to do evil. It may be the exact opposite of testing, which if surmounted, brings spiritual strength and good. One is inspired by Satan (Ephesians 6:11), the other by God (Deuteronomy 8:16, Job 23:10; 1Peter 1:7).

Tithe – The principle of a 10% tax is ancient and not limited to the Bible. Abraham was accustomed to it at the beginning of the second millennium B.C. (Hebrews 7:59). Jacob promised it to God (Genesis 28:22). The tithe of everything was the Lord's, and He gave it as an inheritance to the Levites (Leviticus 27: 30-32). During Roman times, it was still observed by the faithful (Matthew 23:23; Luke 18:12).

Tongues – Speaking in tongues is a genre of prophecy when the speaker speaks prophetically, ecstatically, and miraculously in a language he has not learned. To understand what is being said, the person speaking or another in the church uses the gift of interpretation to translate (1 Corinthians 14: 26-28).

Translation – The process of rendering words and meaning from one language to another.

Tribulation – In both testaments the word refers to trouble, of a general sort, but sometimes as punishment from God. The NT refers in a few cases to a great tribulation (Matthew 24:21, 29; Mark 13:19, 24; Revelation 2:22; 7:14). It will be a time of unparalleled suffering in the end of days.

Victory – This word is often used in a military battle or athletic contest. Christ has success over everything opposed to God – i.e. the world (John 16:33). The Christian can overcome evil with good (Romans 12:21). The resurrection has given believers the victory over death (1 Corinthians 15:54; 1John 2:14; 4:4; 5:4-5).

Vine – The grape is one of the most common plants mentioned in the Bible. It is often used symbolically. Israel was God's vine brought from Egypt and planted in the Promised Land. But she turned out to be a wild vine, and for this had to be punished – cut off. However, then she would grow again and produce fruit fit for the vinedresser (Psalm 80:89; Isaiah 5: 1-7; 65:8-9; Jeremiah 2:21).

Jesus called Himself the "true vine" and His Father the "vinedresser," and His followers the "branches" which must abide in the vine to produce fruit. (John 15: 1-11).

Virgin Birth – The miraculous work that Jesus Christ was born of Mary without being conceived through sexual intercourse. The Holy Spirit was the source of conception (Matthew 1: 18).

Walk – A word describing how one lives his life. It relates to one's conduct in life. Christians are to "walk" worthy of their calling (Ephesians 4:1; Philippians 3: 17-18; Colossians 1: 10; 1Thessalonians 2:12).

Will of God – This involves God's wishes, resolves, wants, and desires. God's exact will for the Christian life includes His desires made know in His Word. His *will* will not take one outside of the commands and principles of His Word.

Wineskin – A leather pouch made from goat or sheep skins that held liquid. The image was used by Jesus to indicate that Christianity would not simply be an offshoot of Pharisaism, but a whole new thing (Matthew 9:17).

Wisdom – An attribute of God, and a quality of the mind of man which makes him wise and skilled (Jeremiah 10:9; Romans 11: 33-36). The fear of the Lord is declared to be the beginning of wisdom (Proverbs 9:10). In the NT Christ is called the wisdom of God and the source of our wisdom (1Corithians 1:24, 30)

Wrath of God – God's justice cannot permit some to obey and others to disobey without an expression of displeasure. His holiness cannot accept sin and evil in His subjects without a reaction of negation and an attempt to correct thereby. As justice and holiness are among the infinite, eternal, unchangeable parts of His being, so must be His wrath.

Yeast – The NIV usually translates the word "unleavened" as "without yeast." It is a substance added to bread dough or liquids to produce fermentation. It is used to illustrate several negative principles: bad influence in Galatians 5:9; the hard-to-understand saying in Mark 8:15; the doctrine of the Pharisees and Sadducees in Matthew 16:6; and hypocrisy in Luke 12:1.

www.ingramcontent.com/pod-product-compliance
Lightning Source LLC
Chambersburg PA
CBHW031327040426
42443CB00005B/250